I am grateful to God, the reason for my existence. I am grateful to my beloved wife, my daughter and my father who is today in glory in the arms of the Father. I am grateful to my daughter-in-law, my son-in-law and my grandchildren. I am grateful to you for purchasing this book. God be praised!

ILTON MORAES

2024

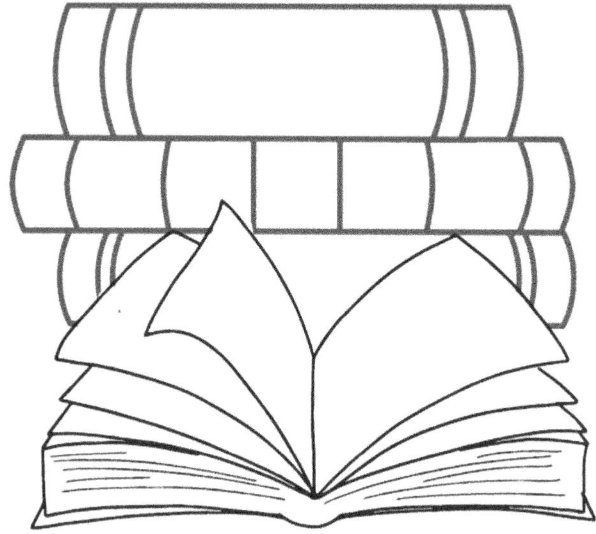

This Book Belongs to:

your name here

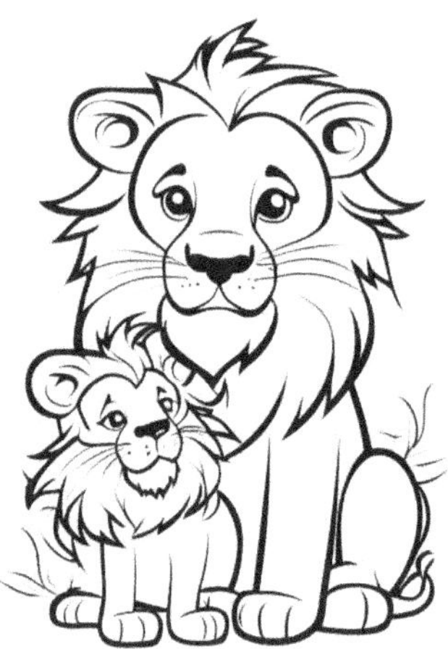

Test Color Page

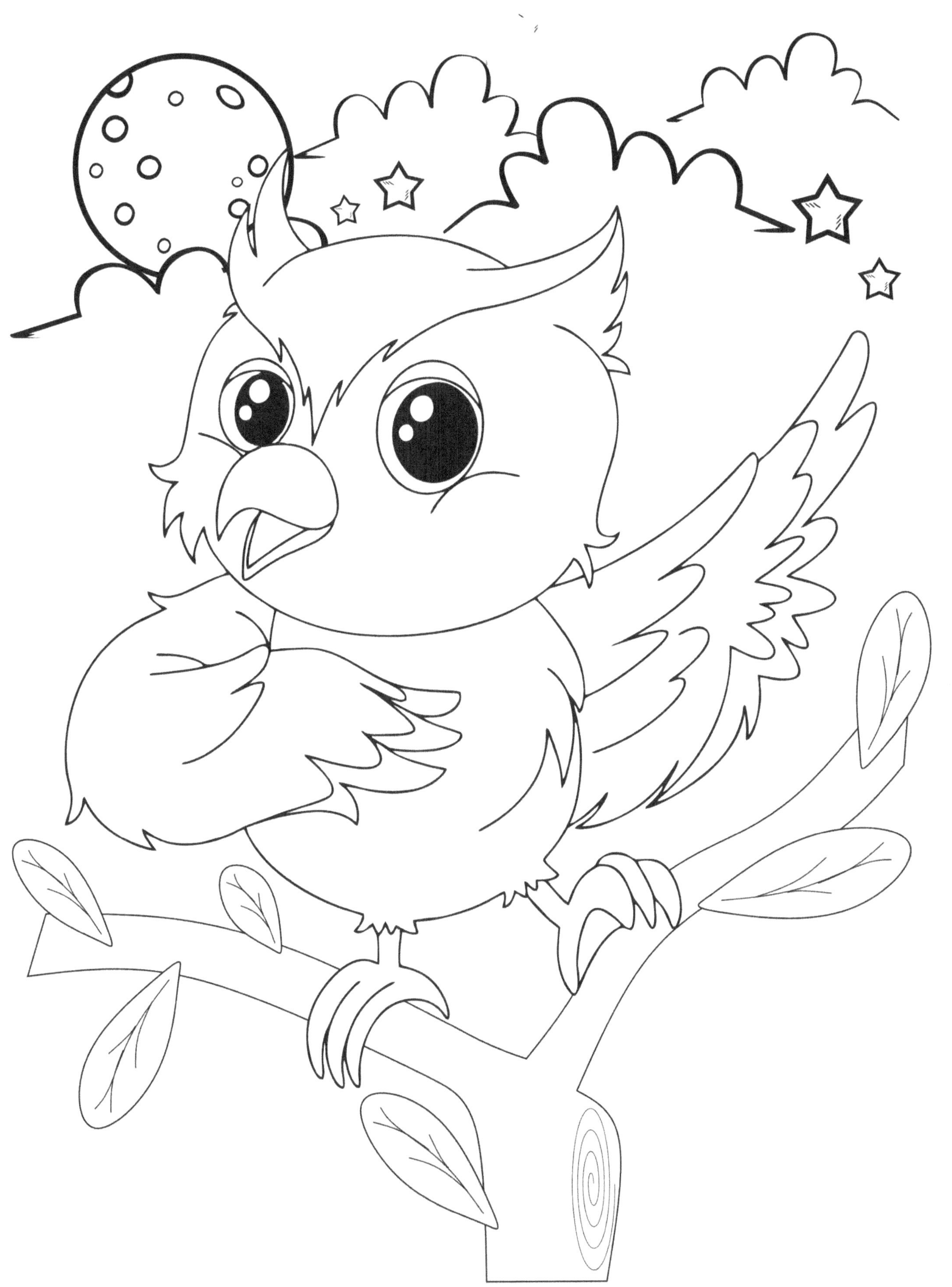

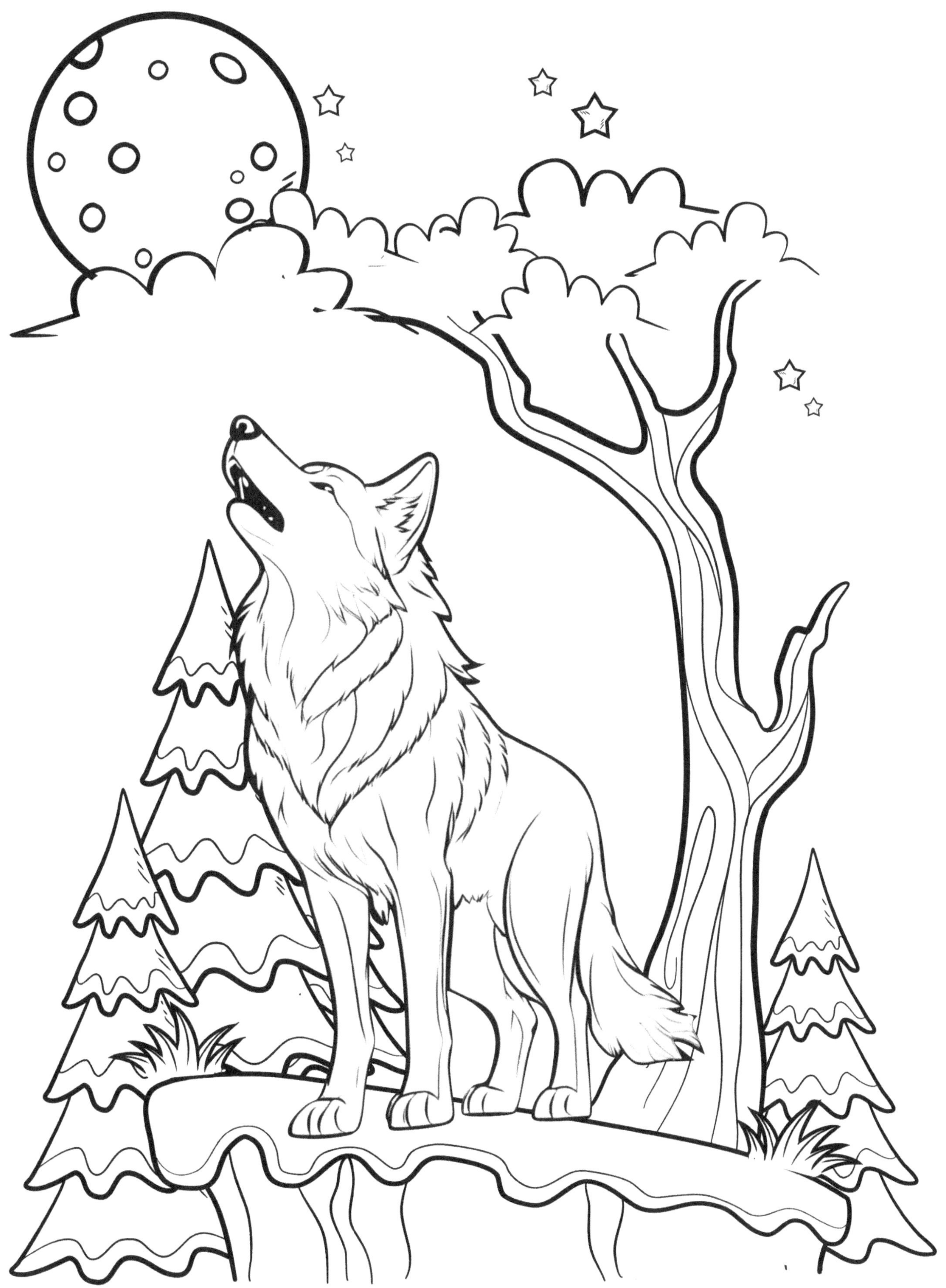

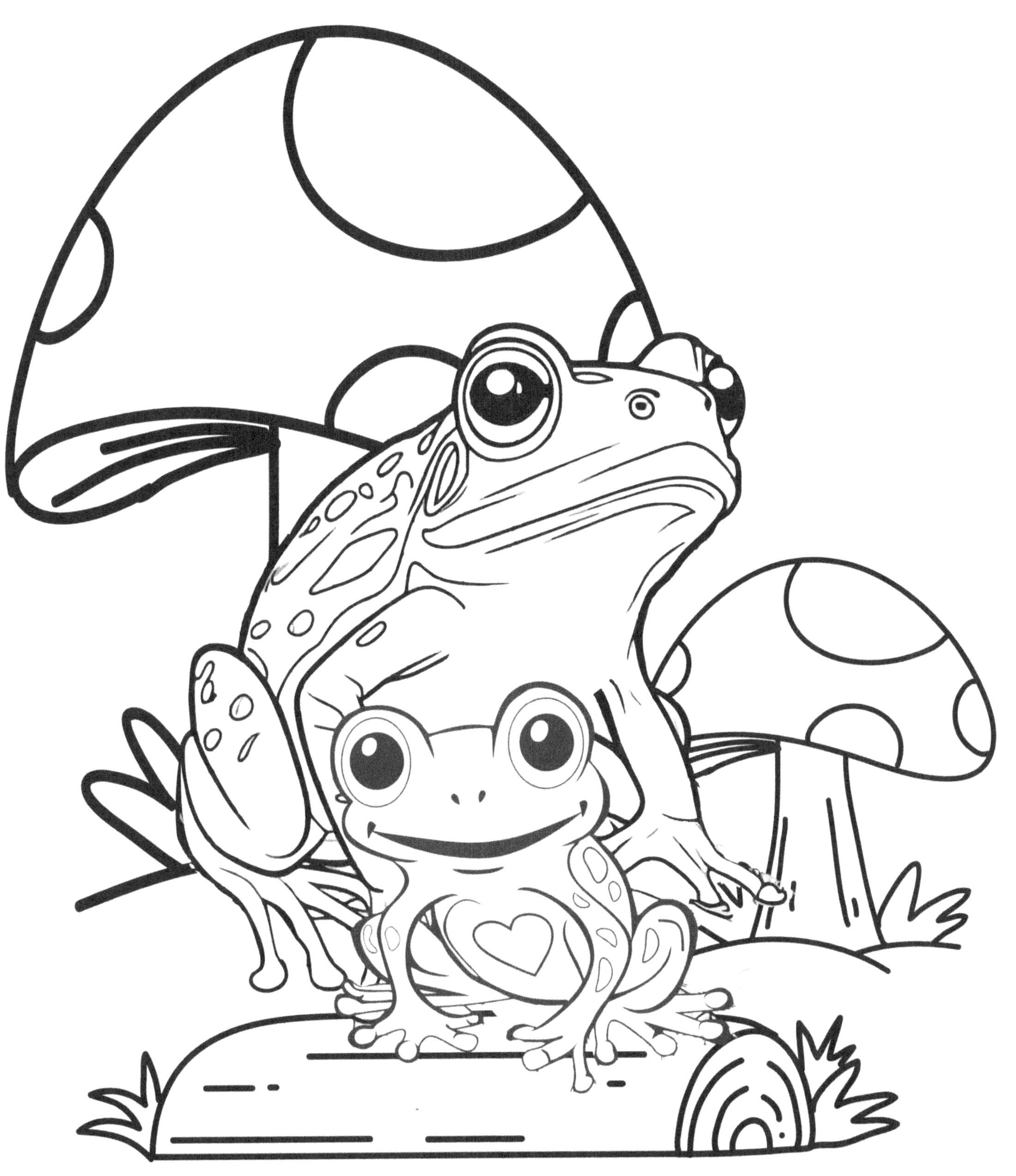

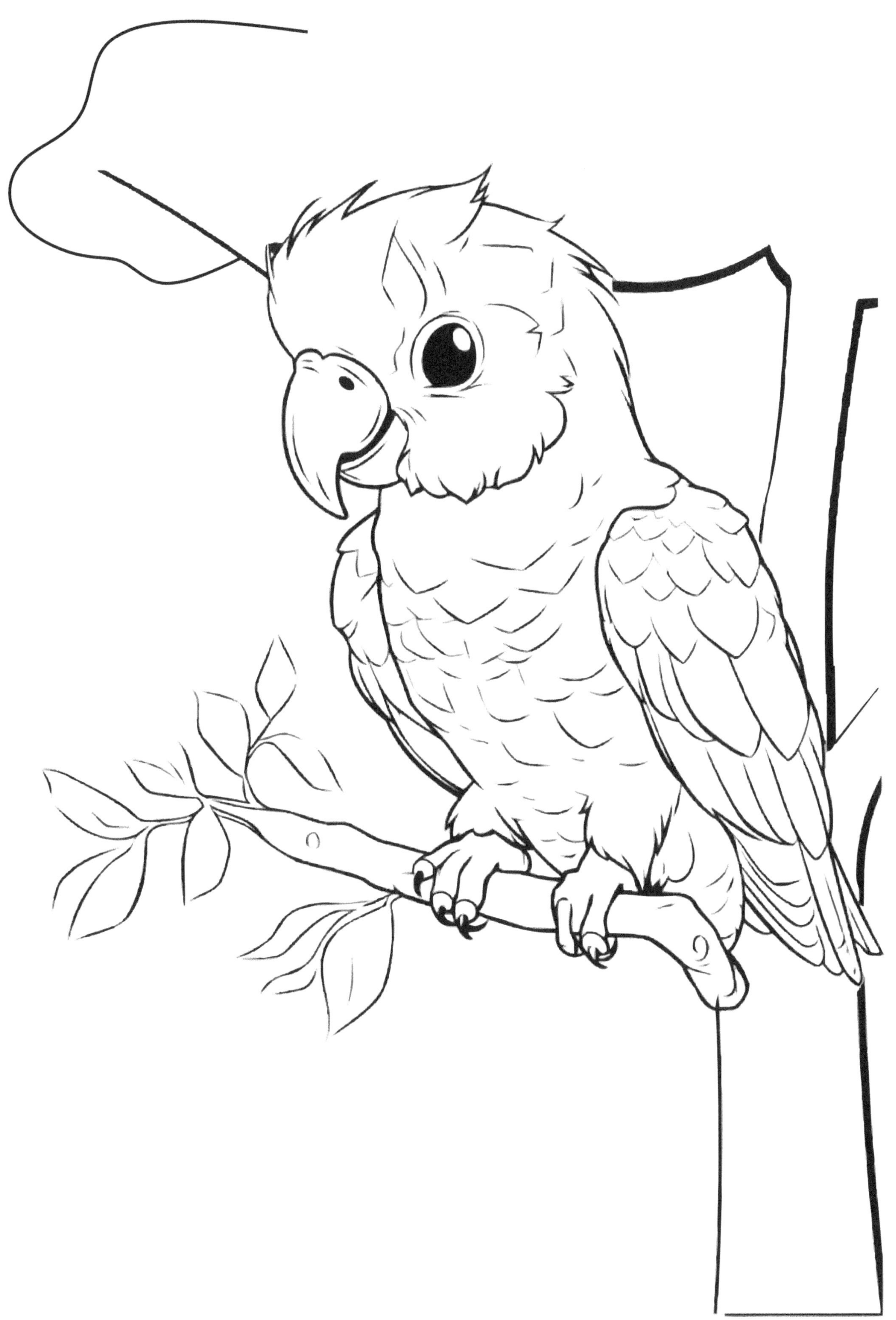

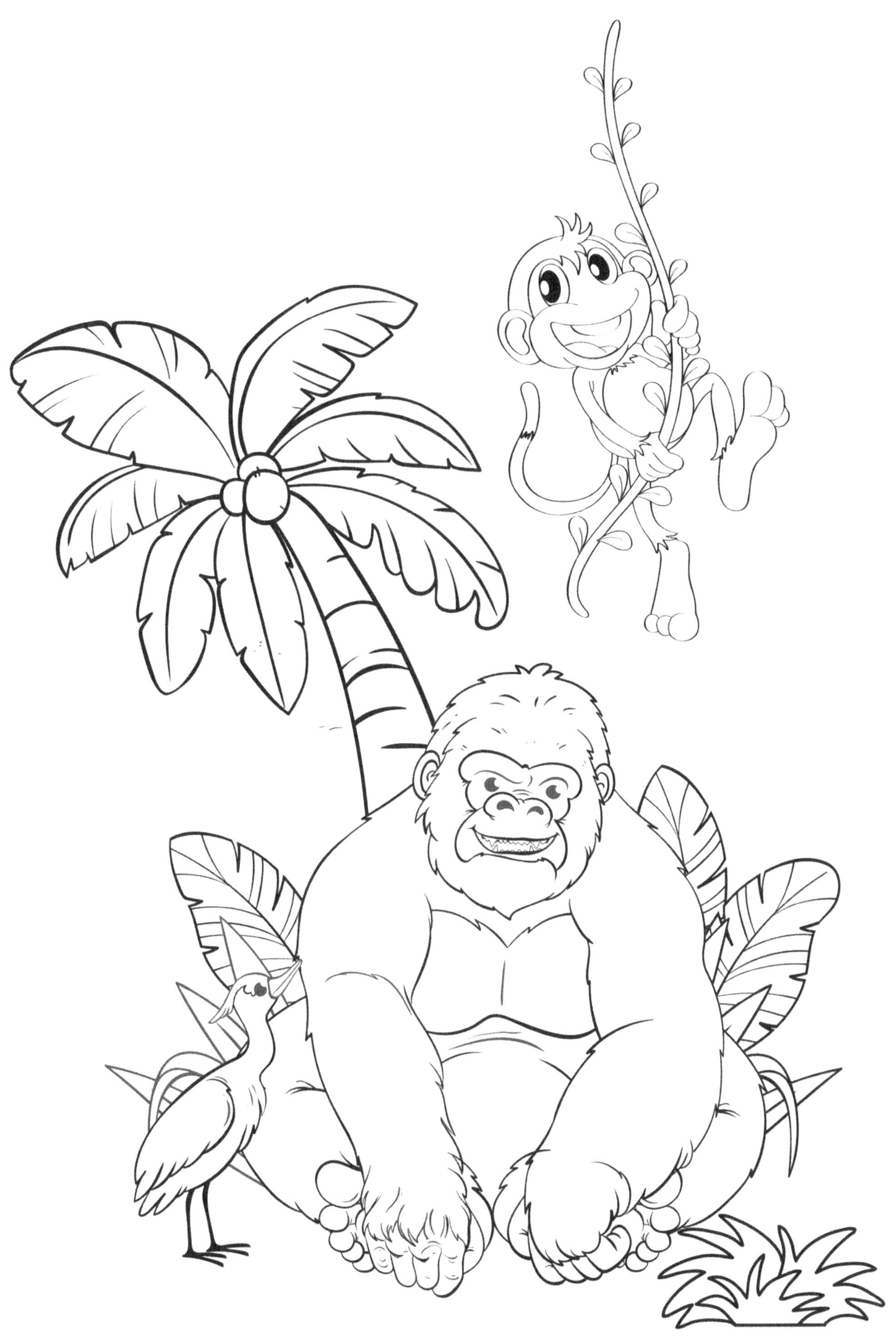

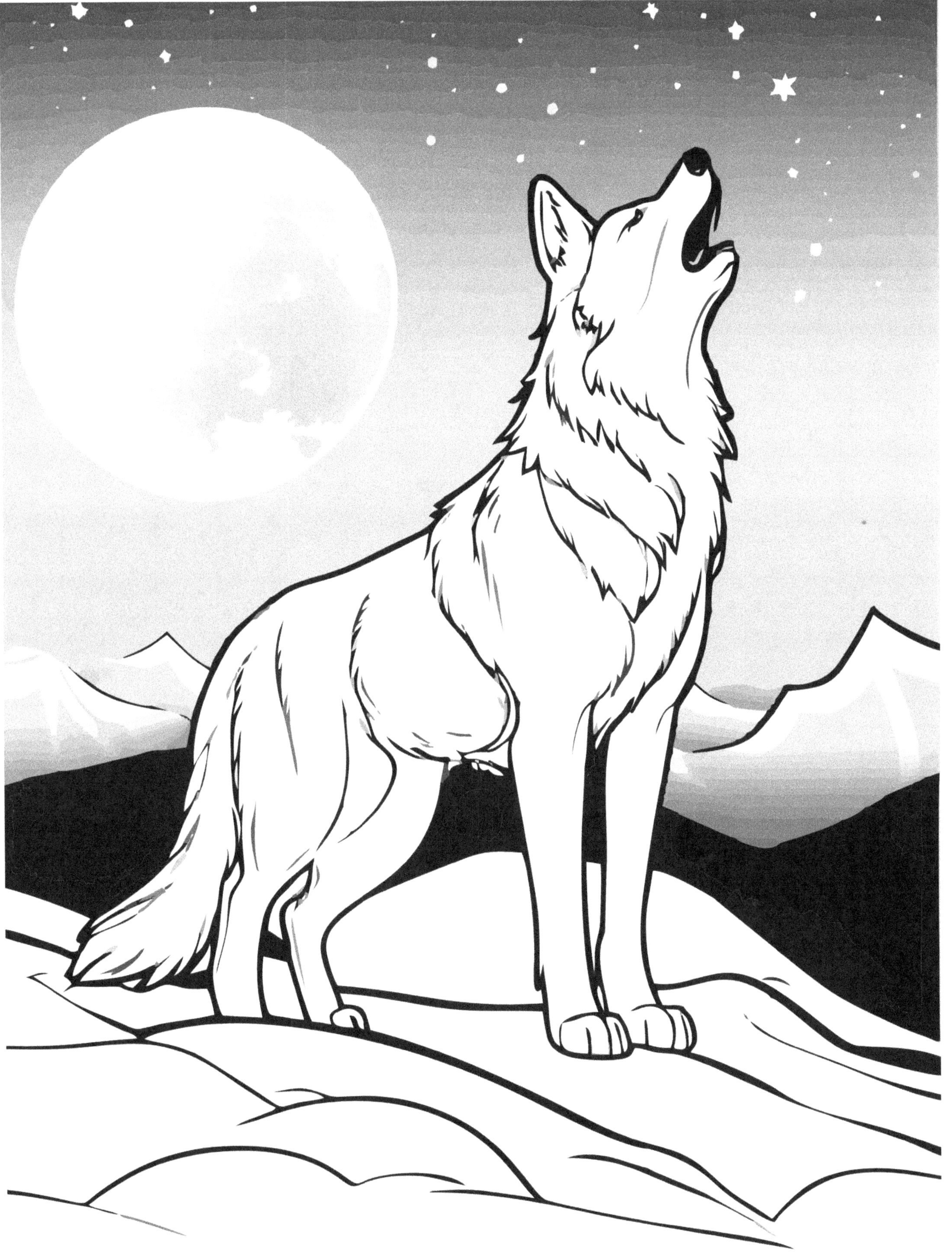

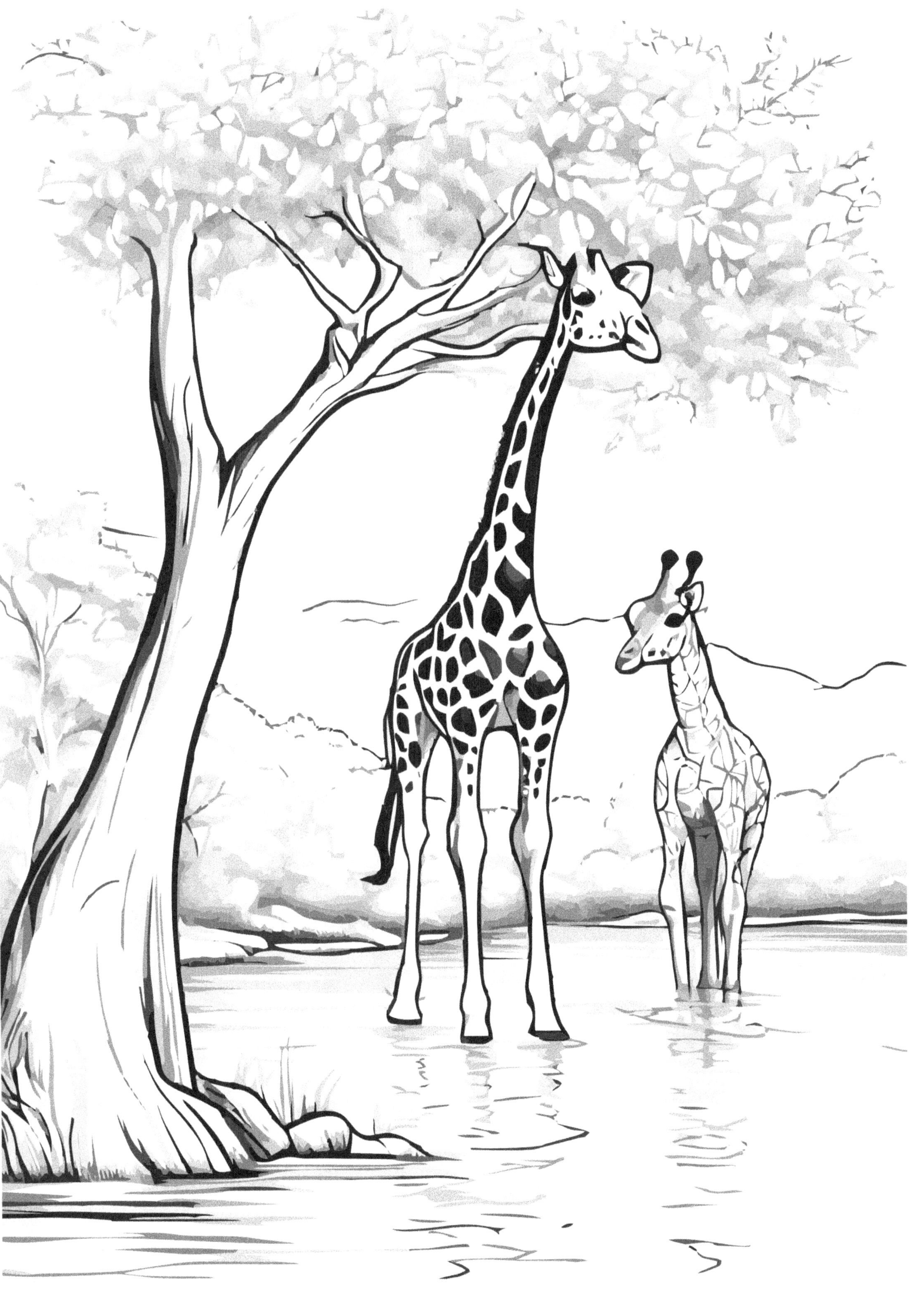

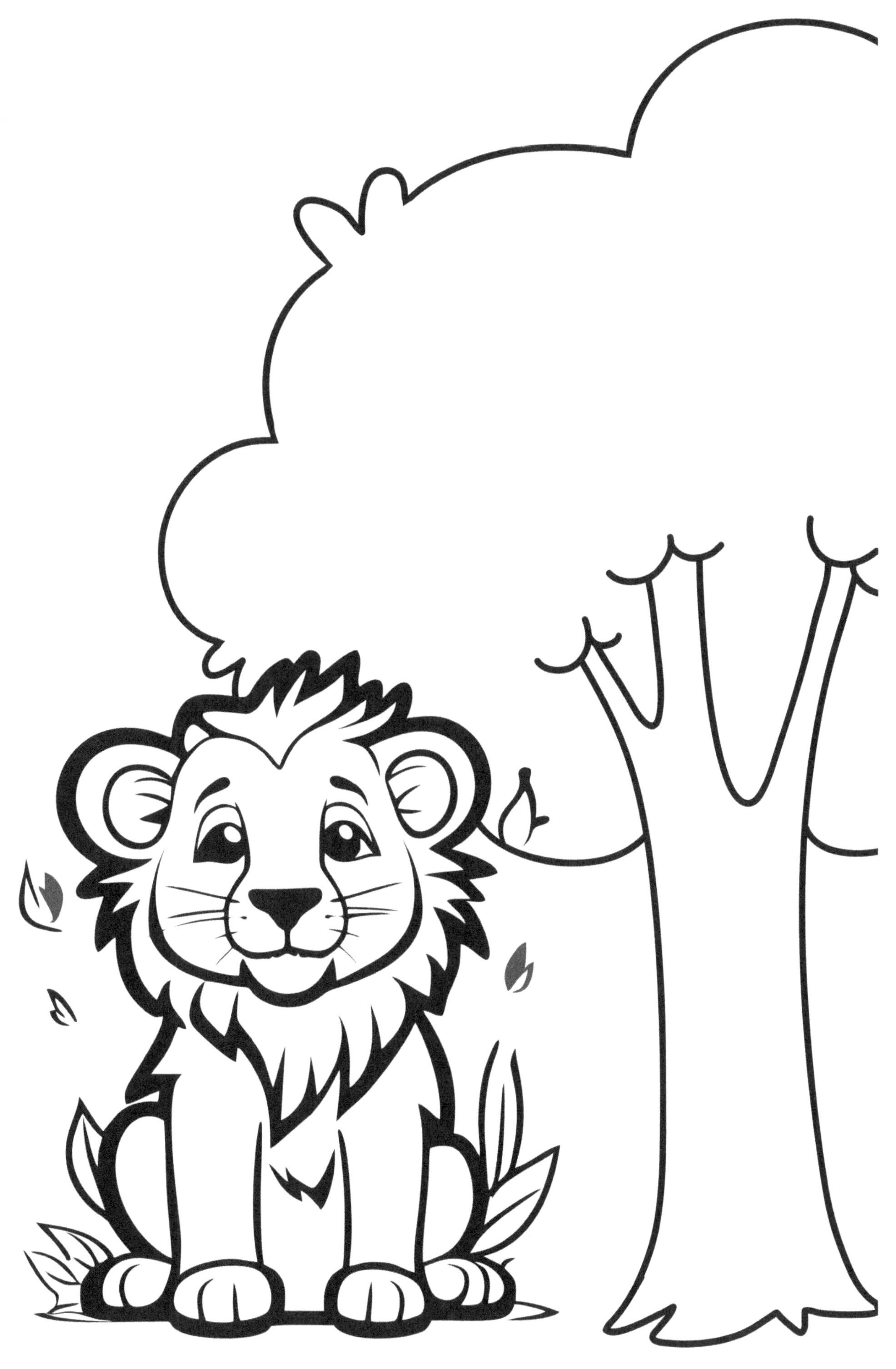

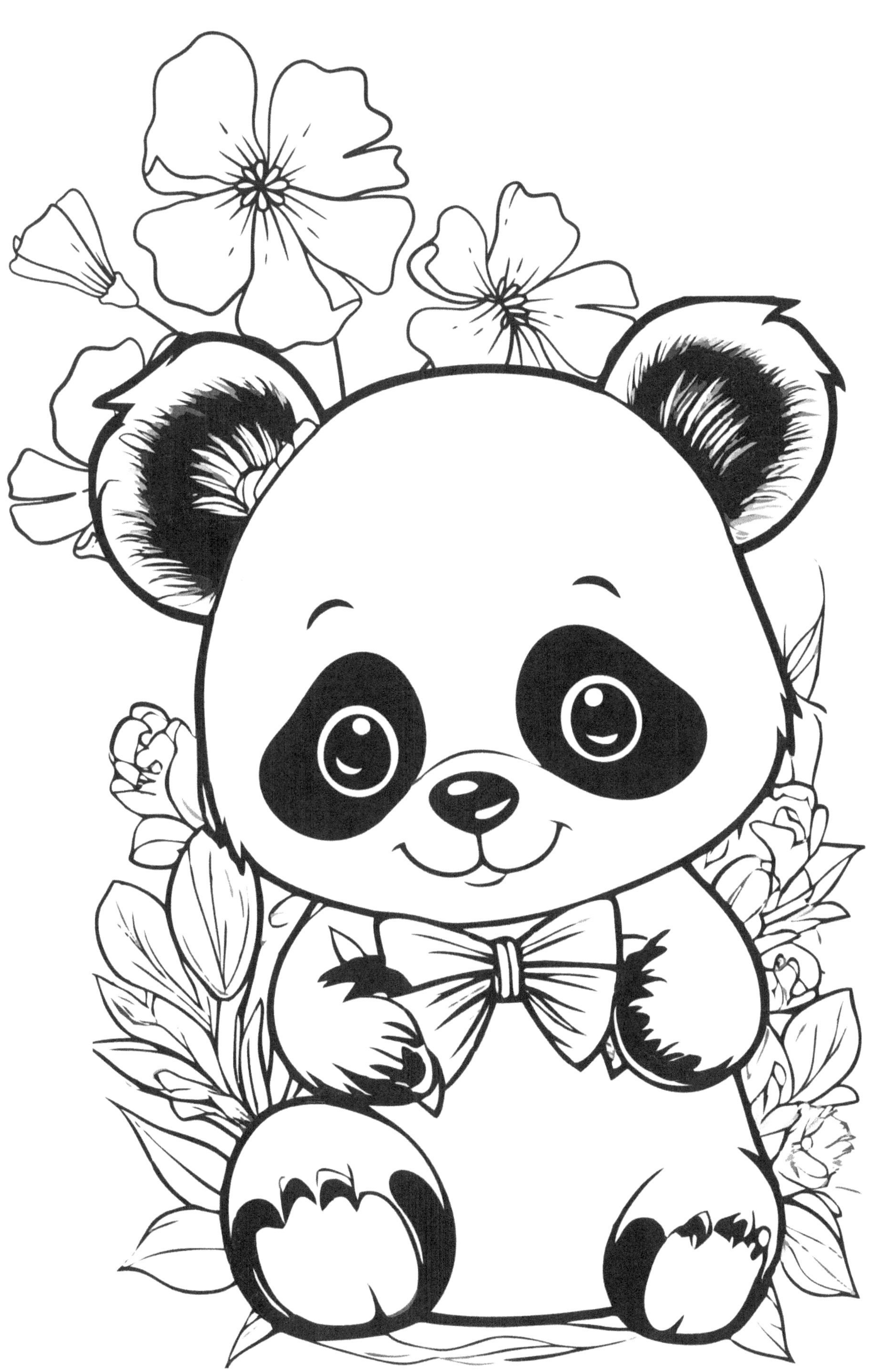

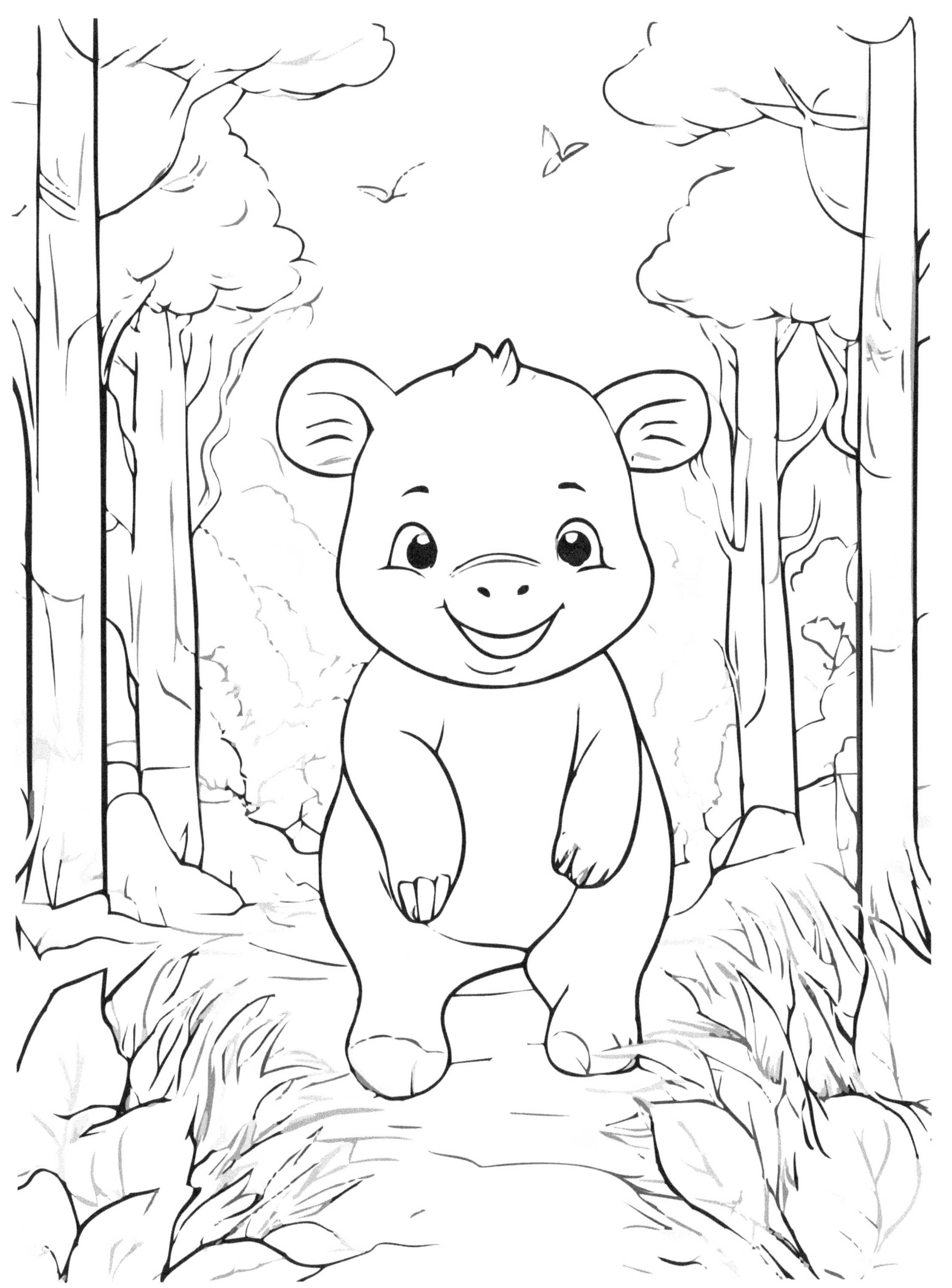

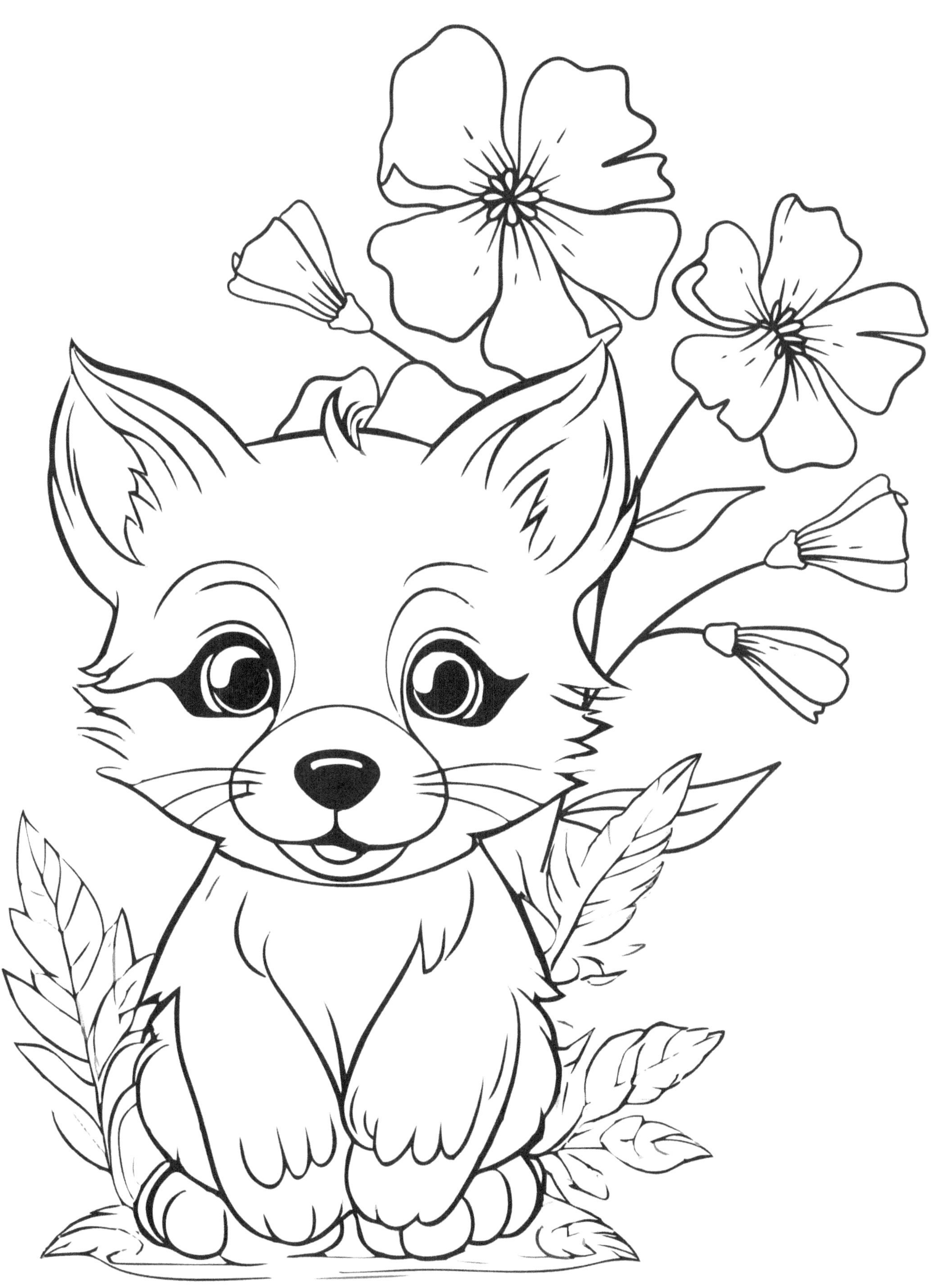

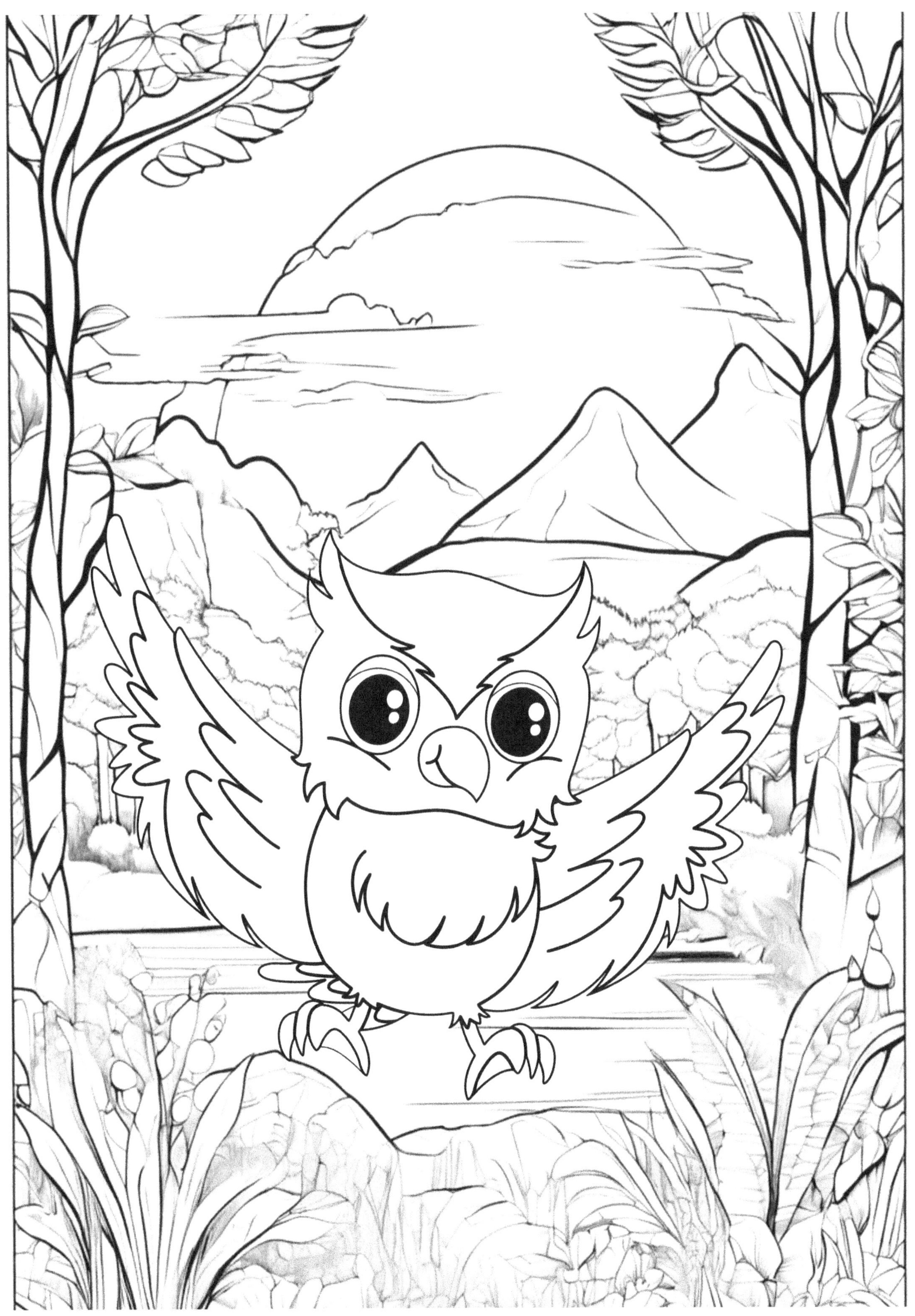

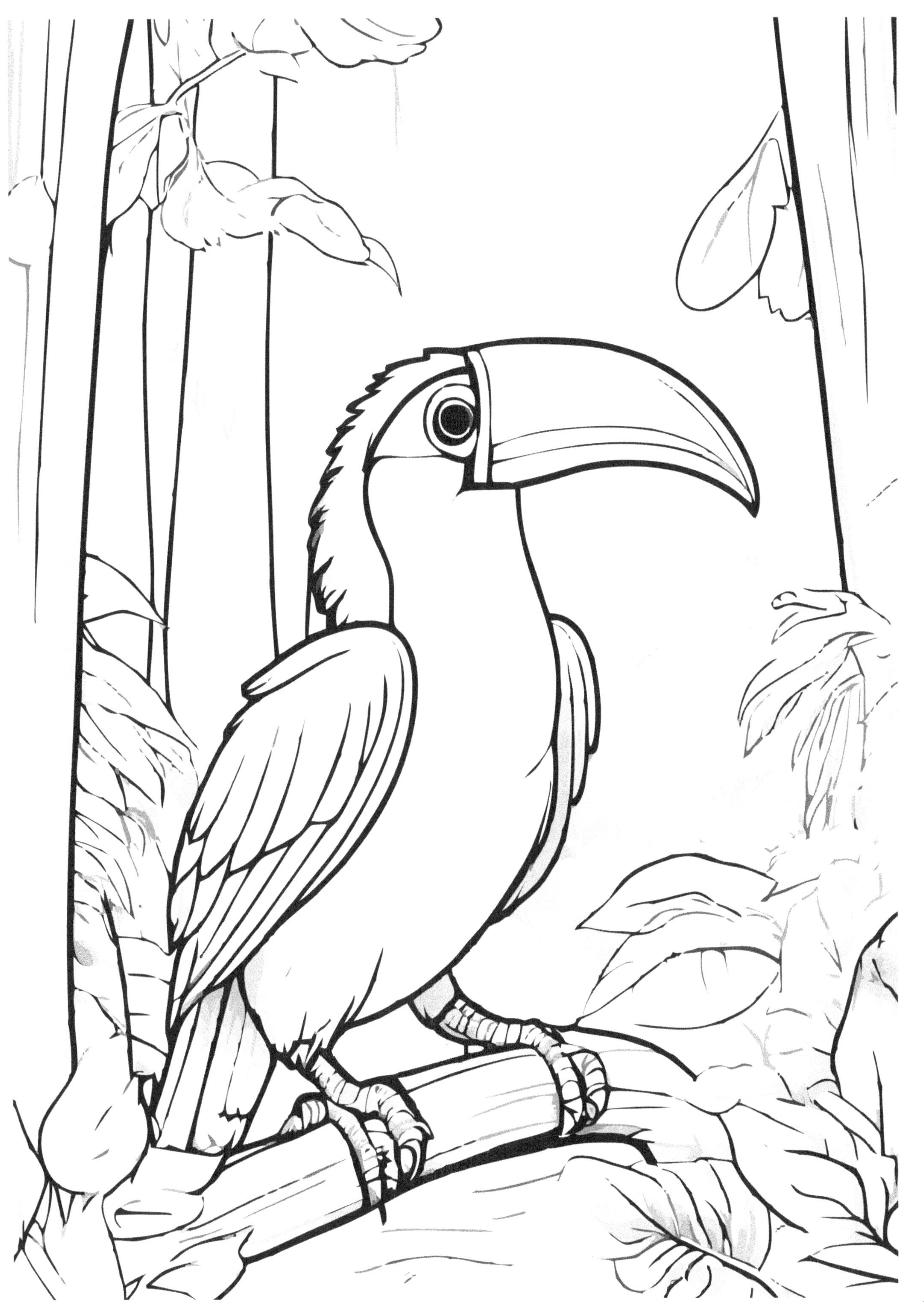

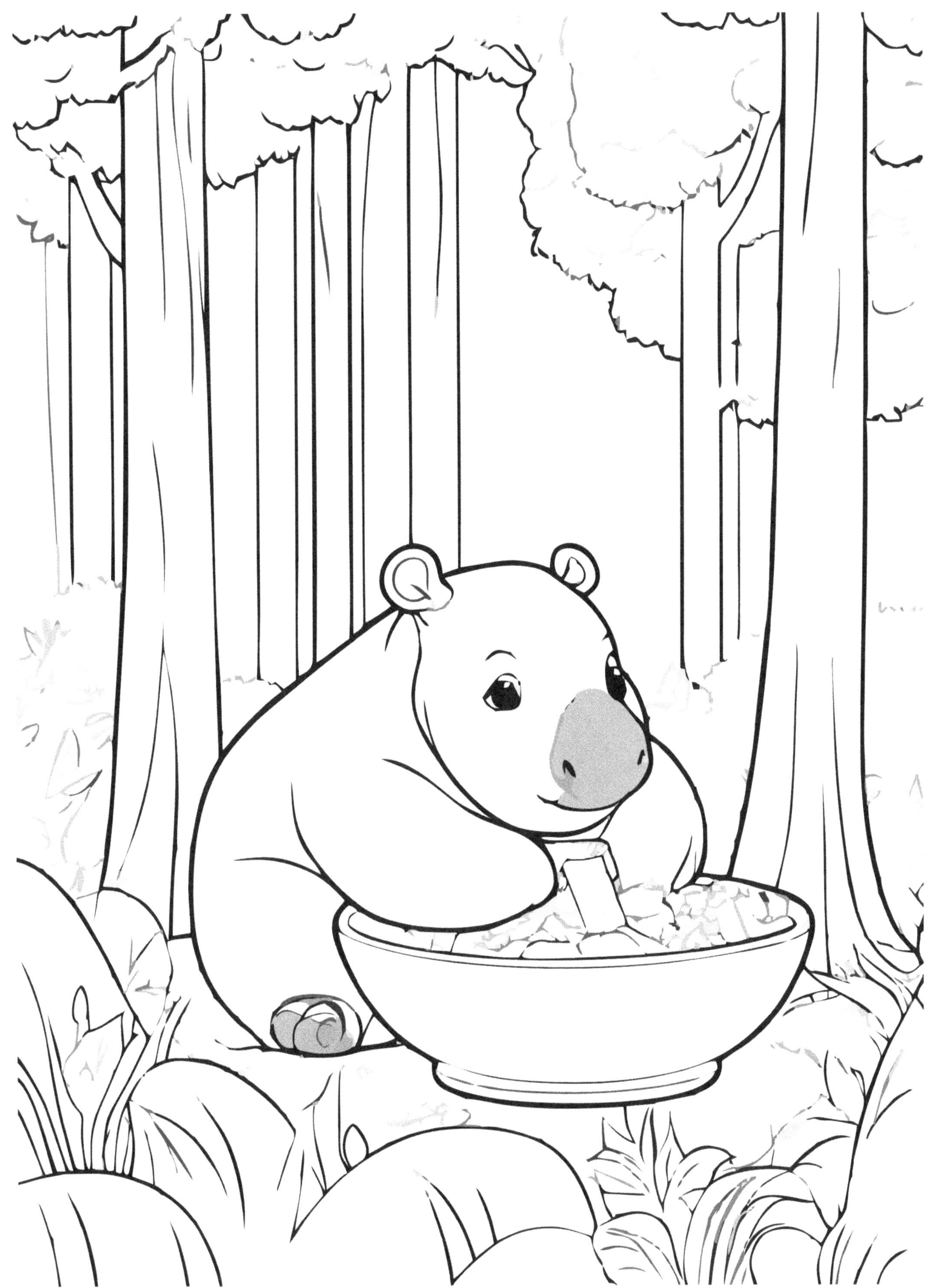

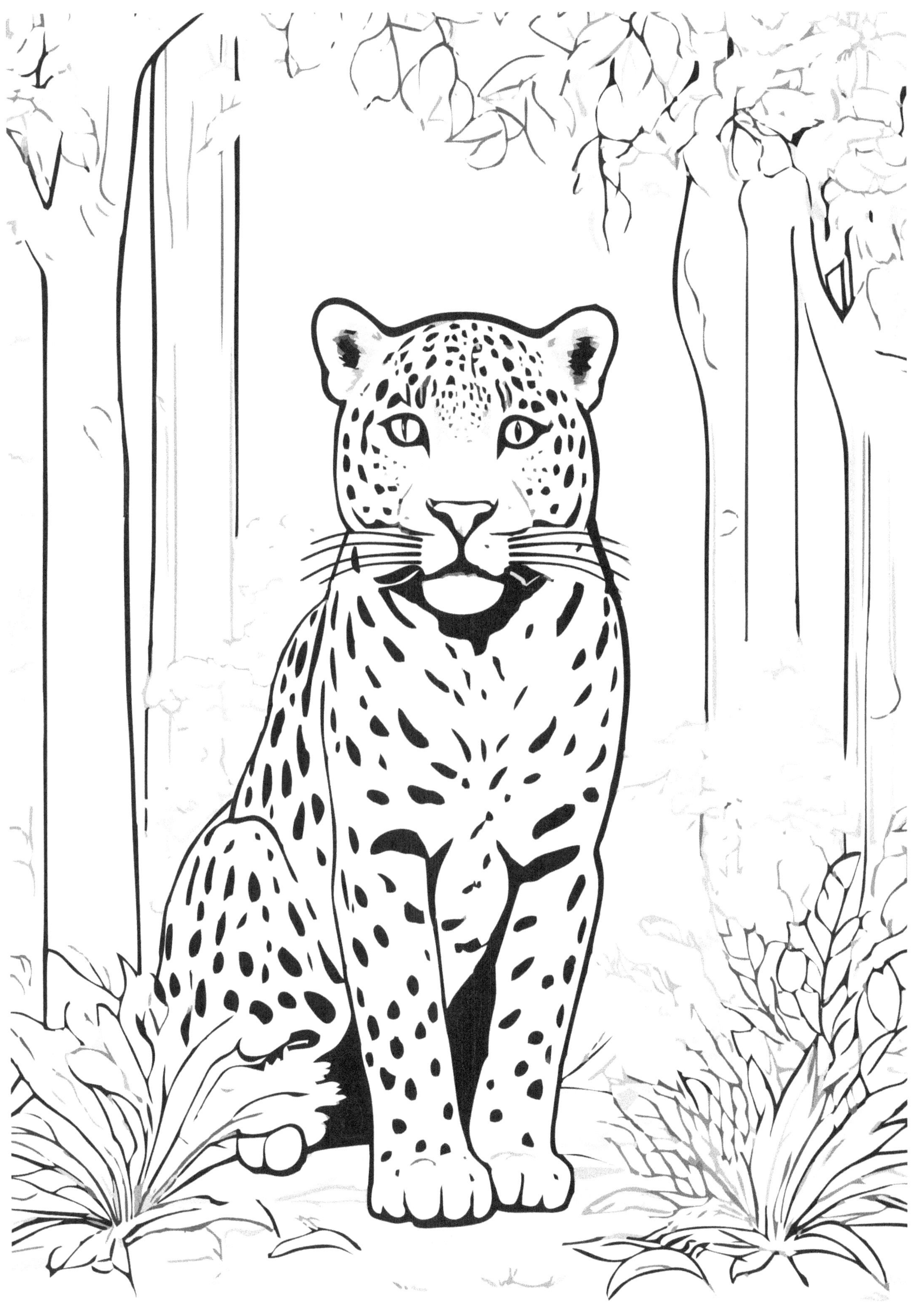

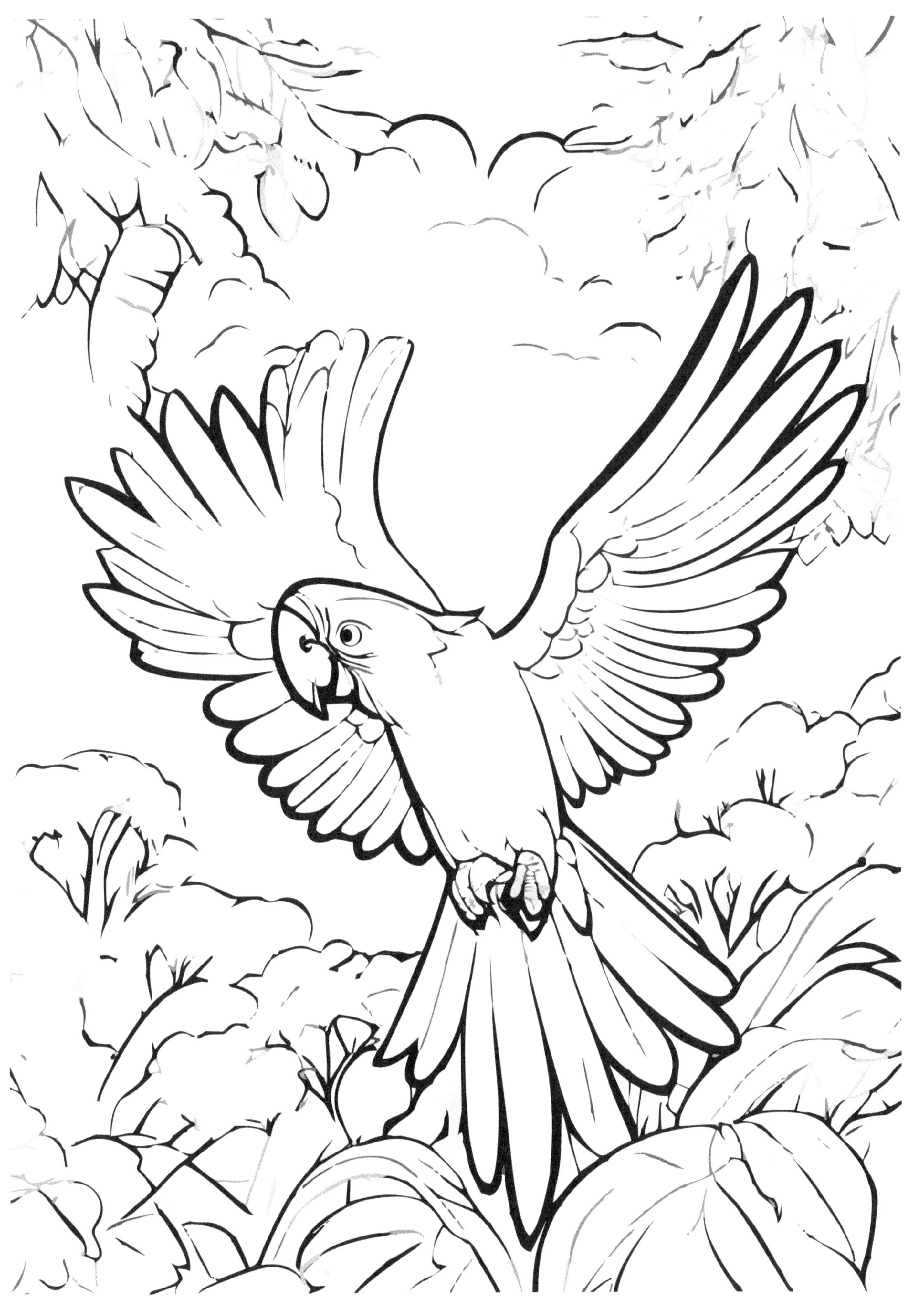

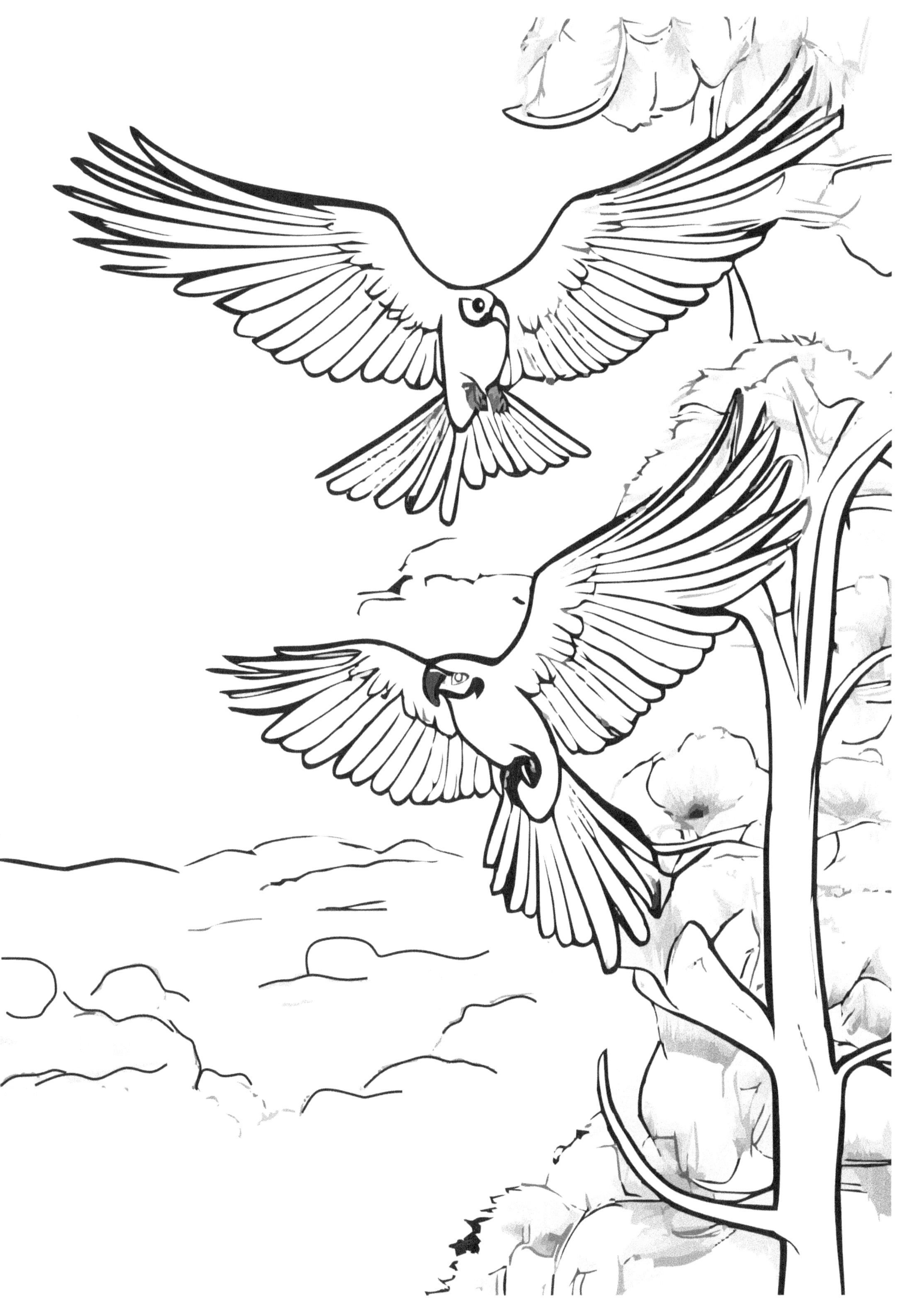

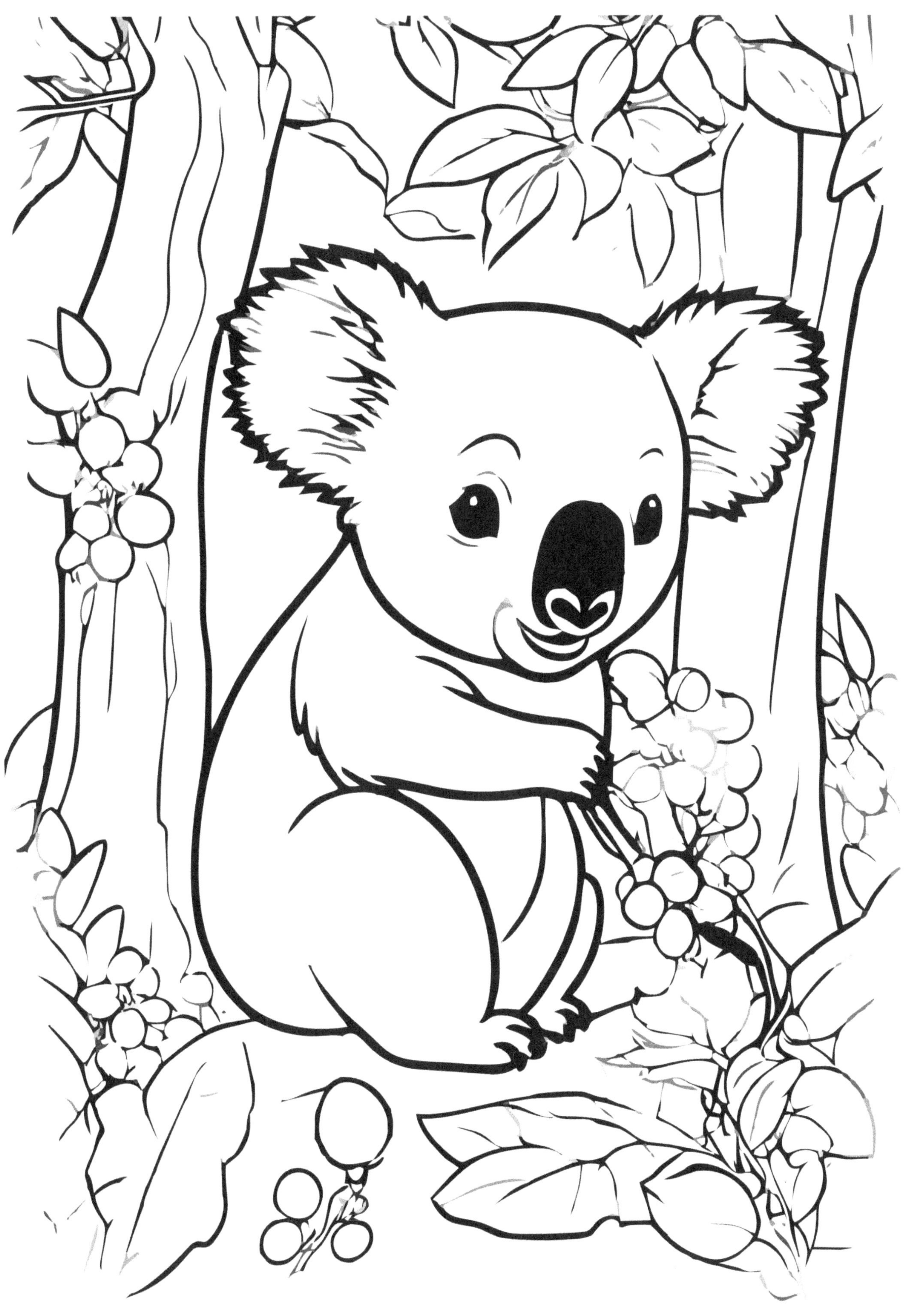

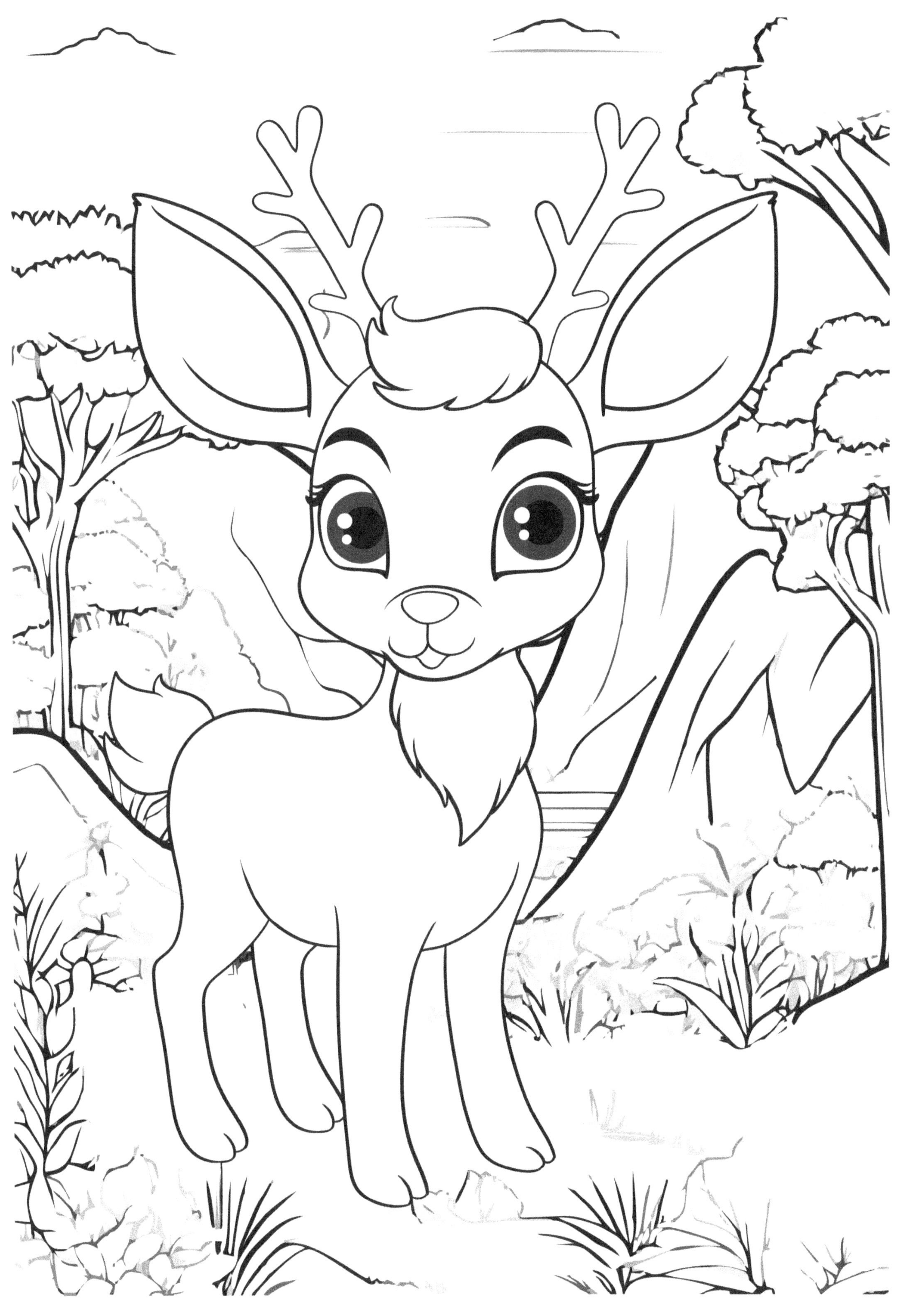

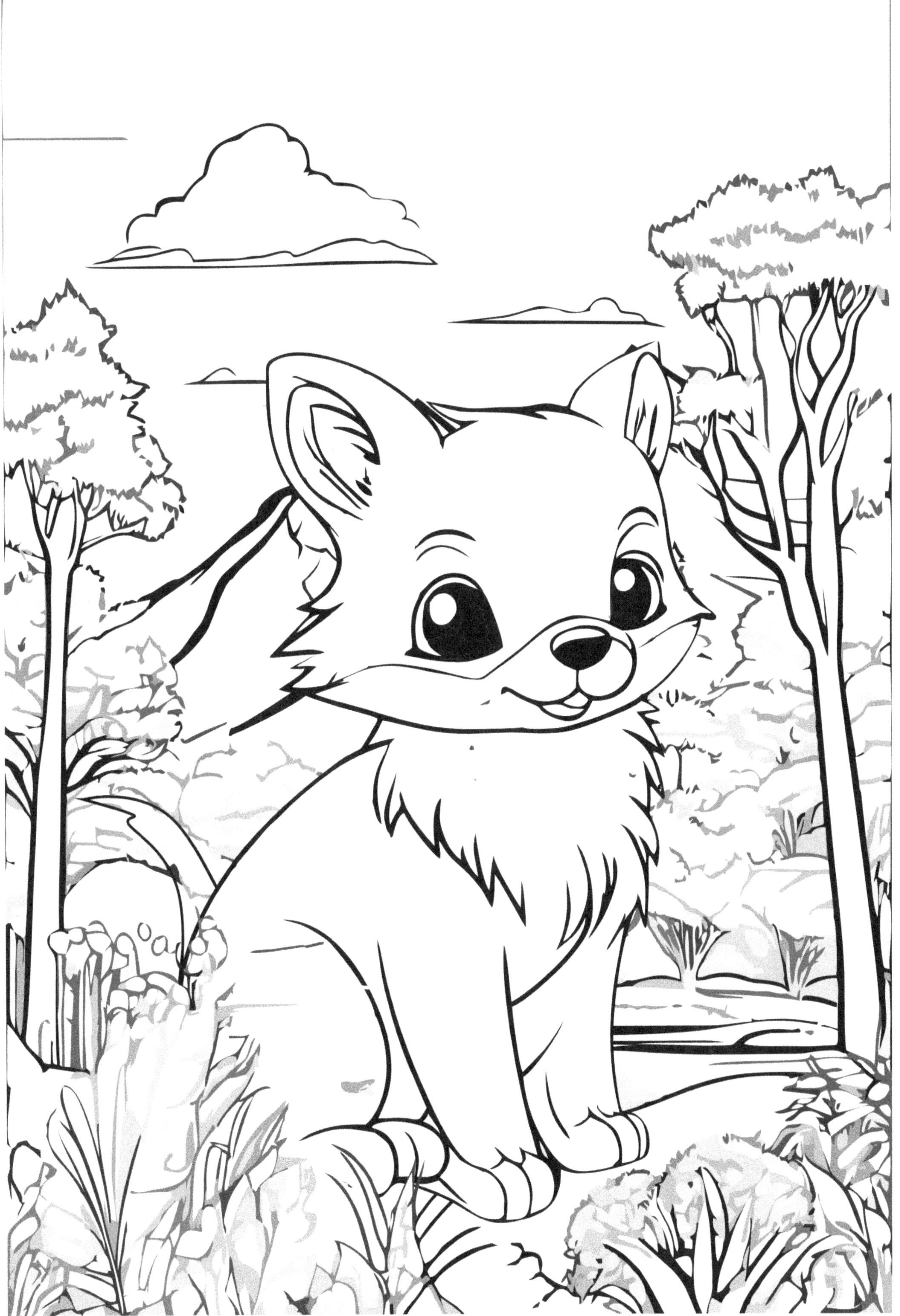

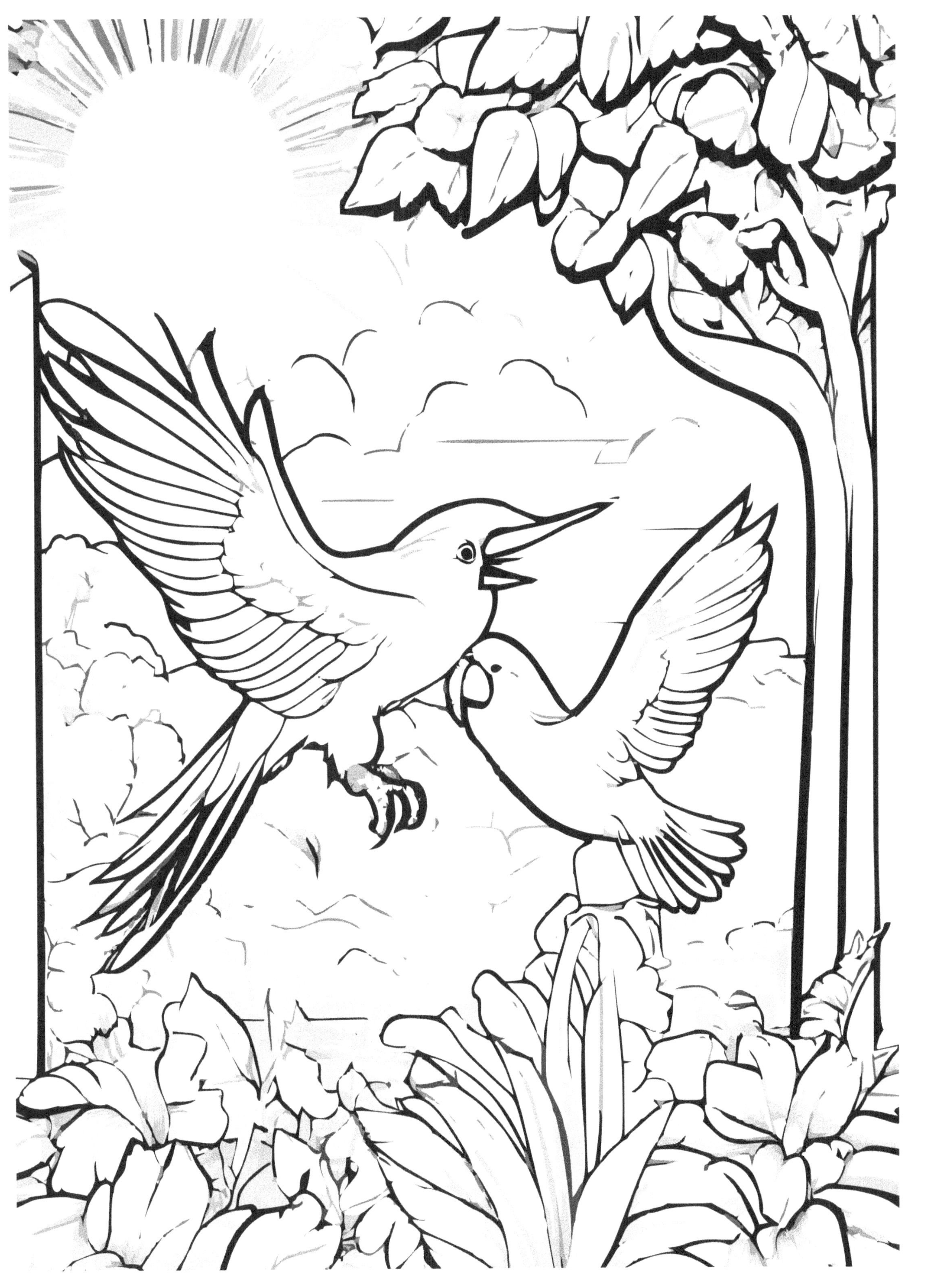

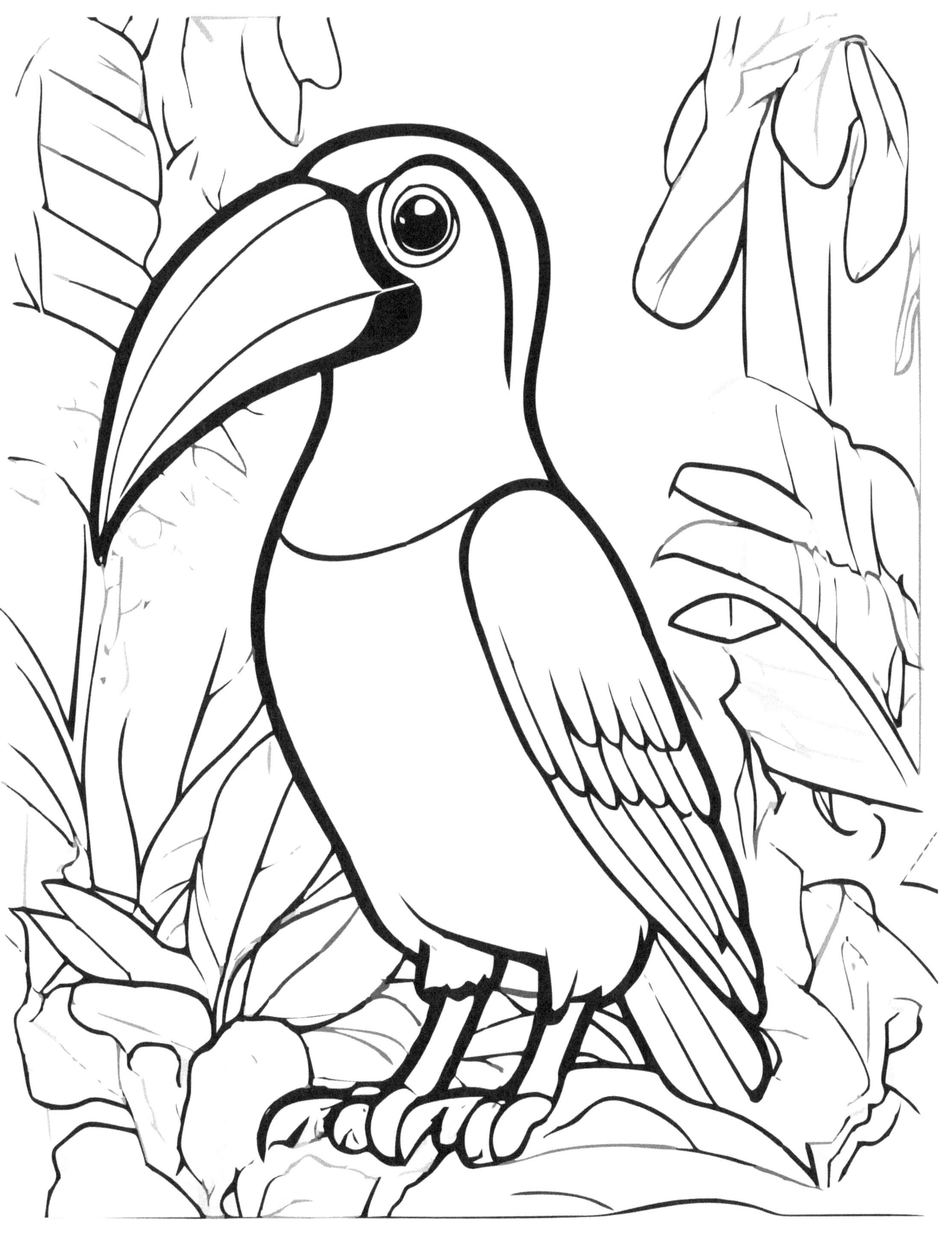

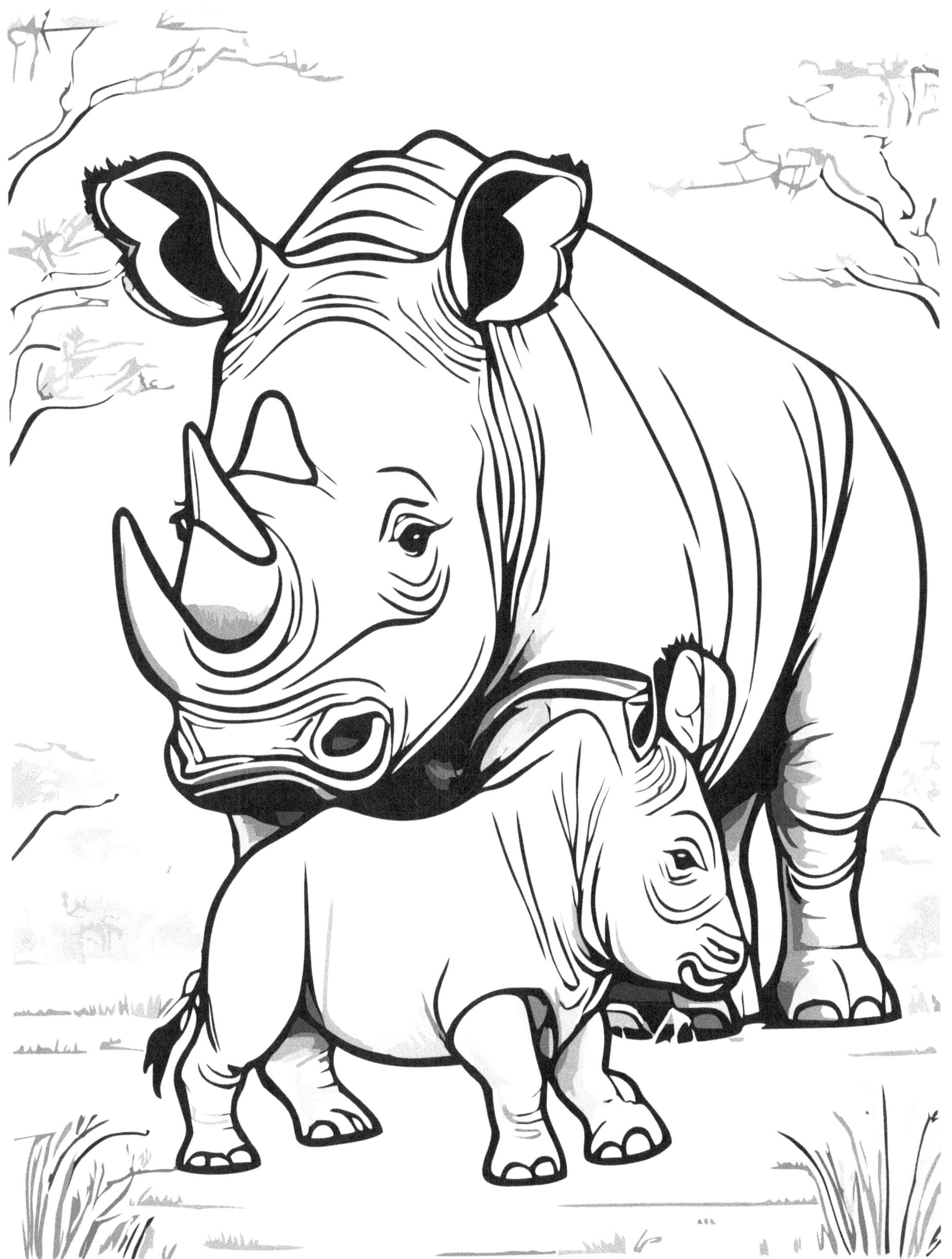

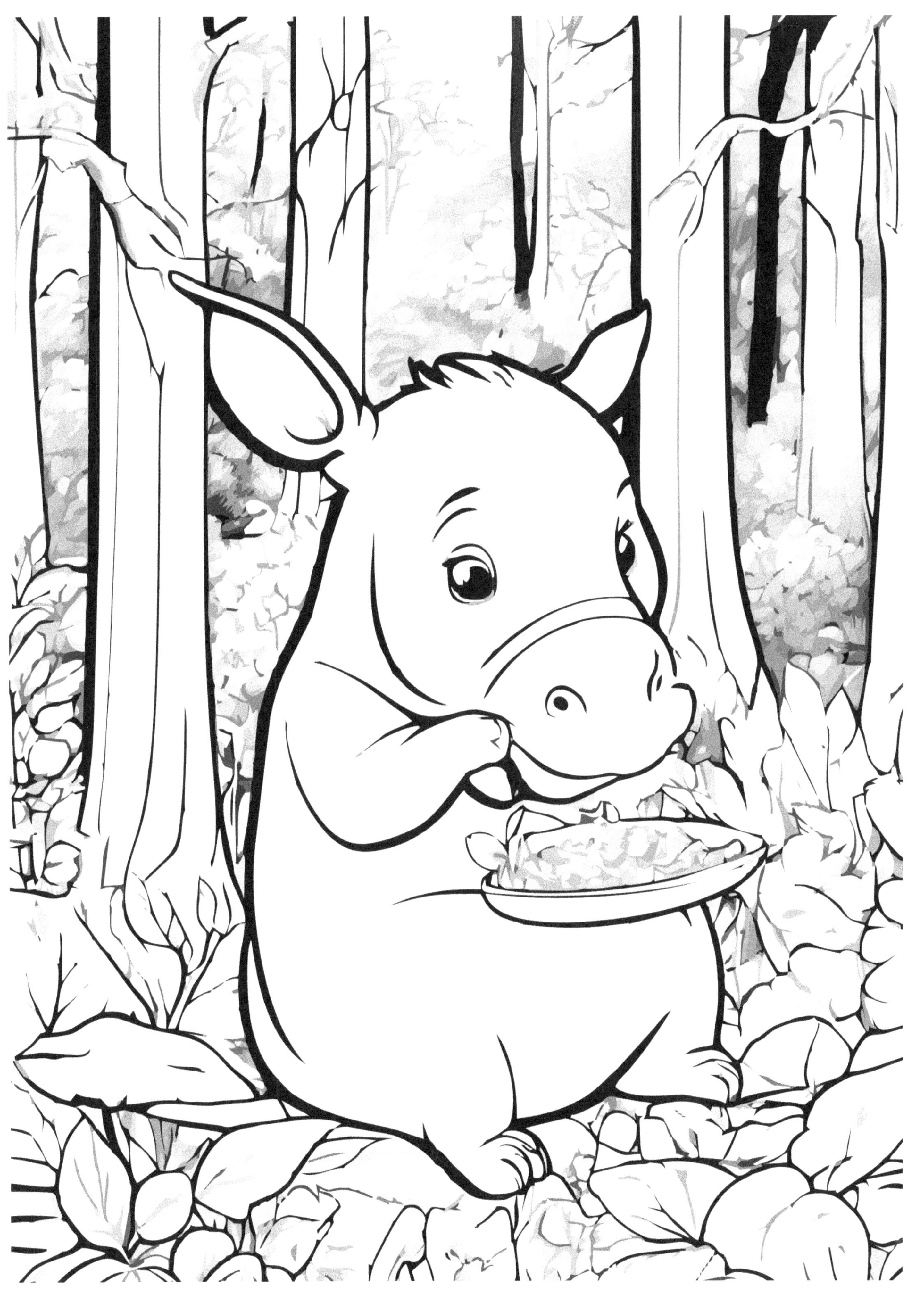

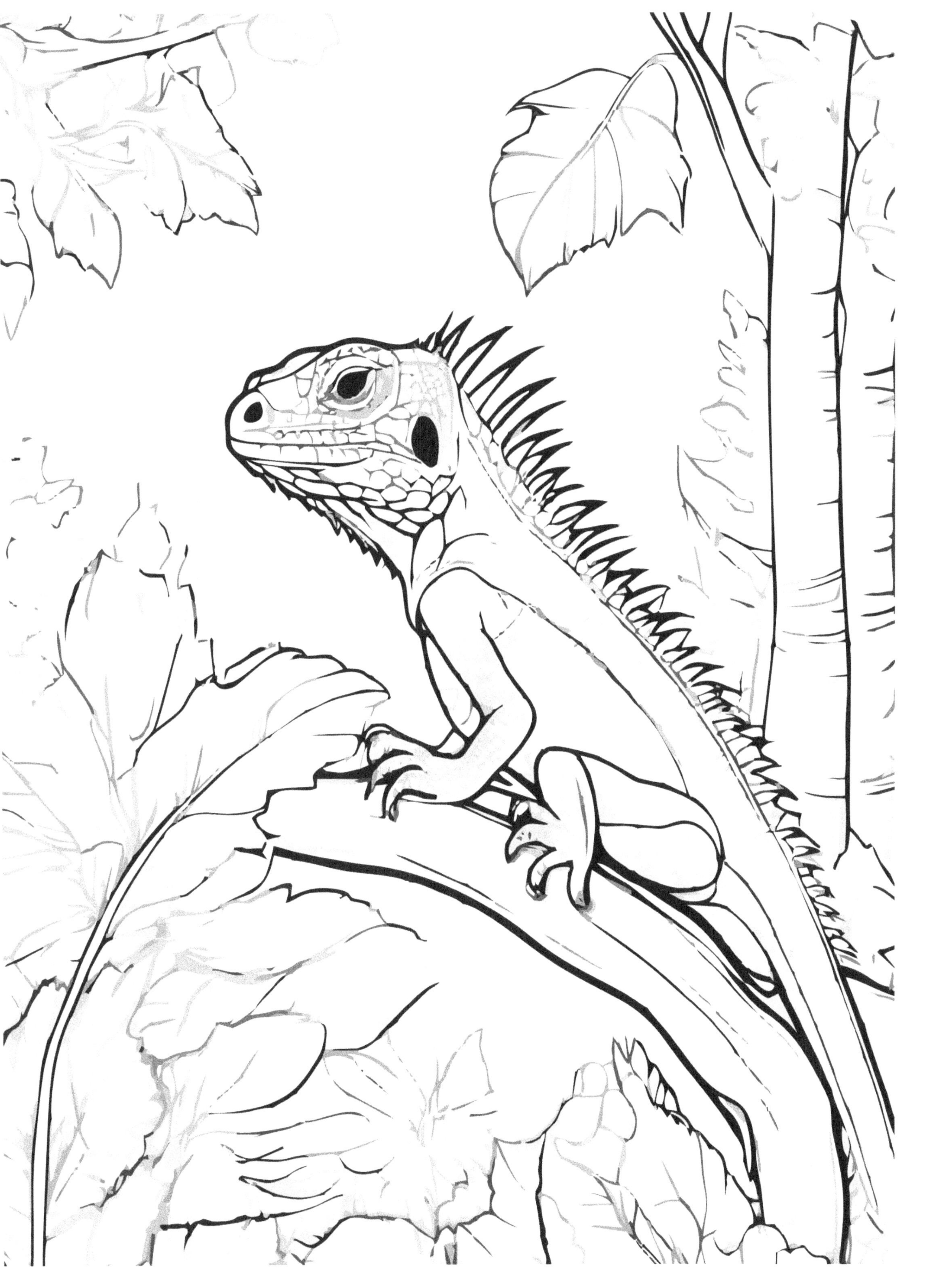

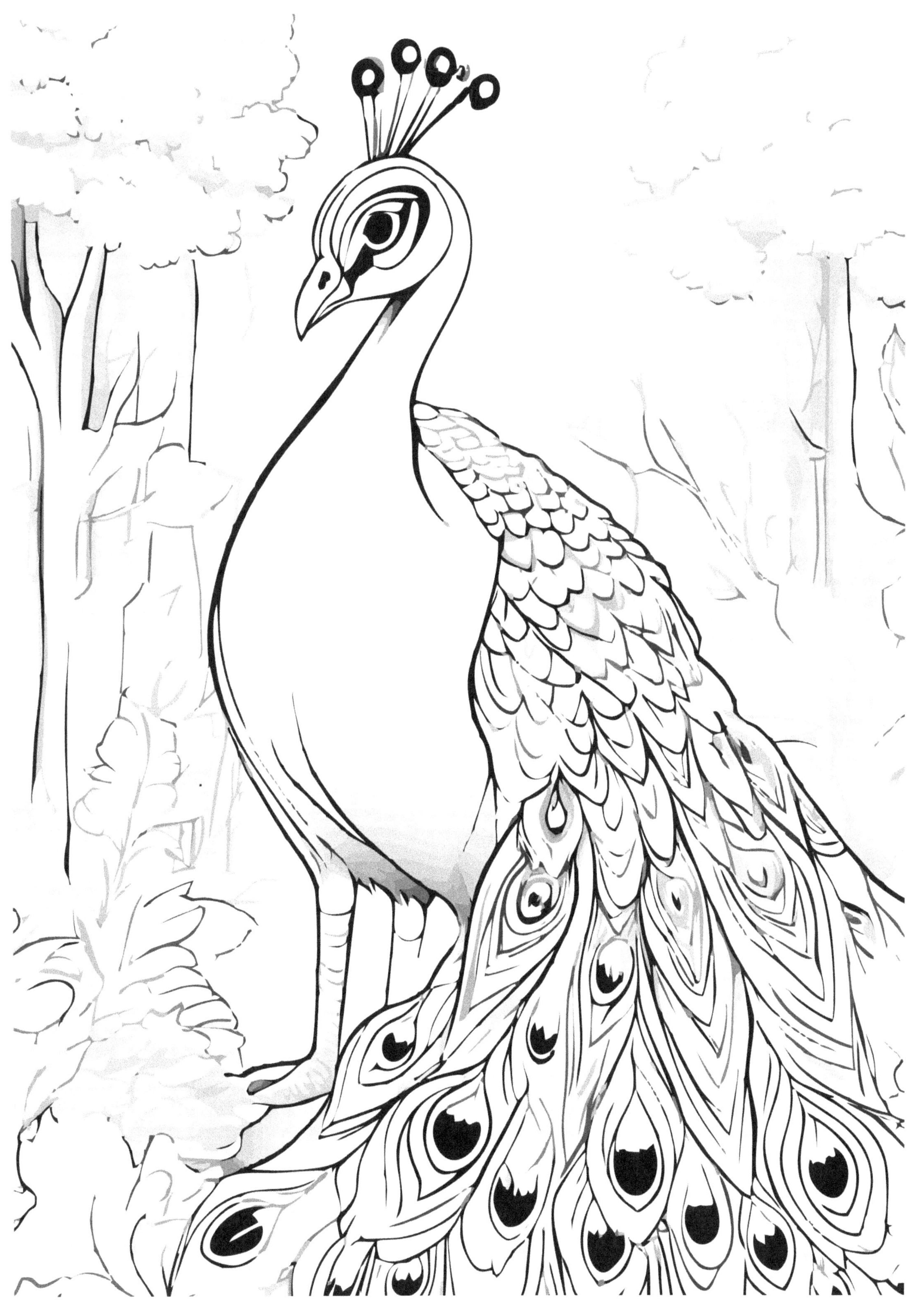

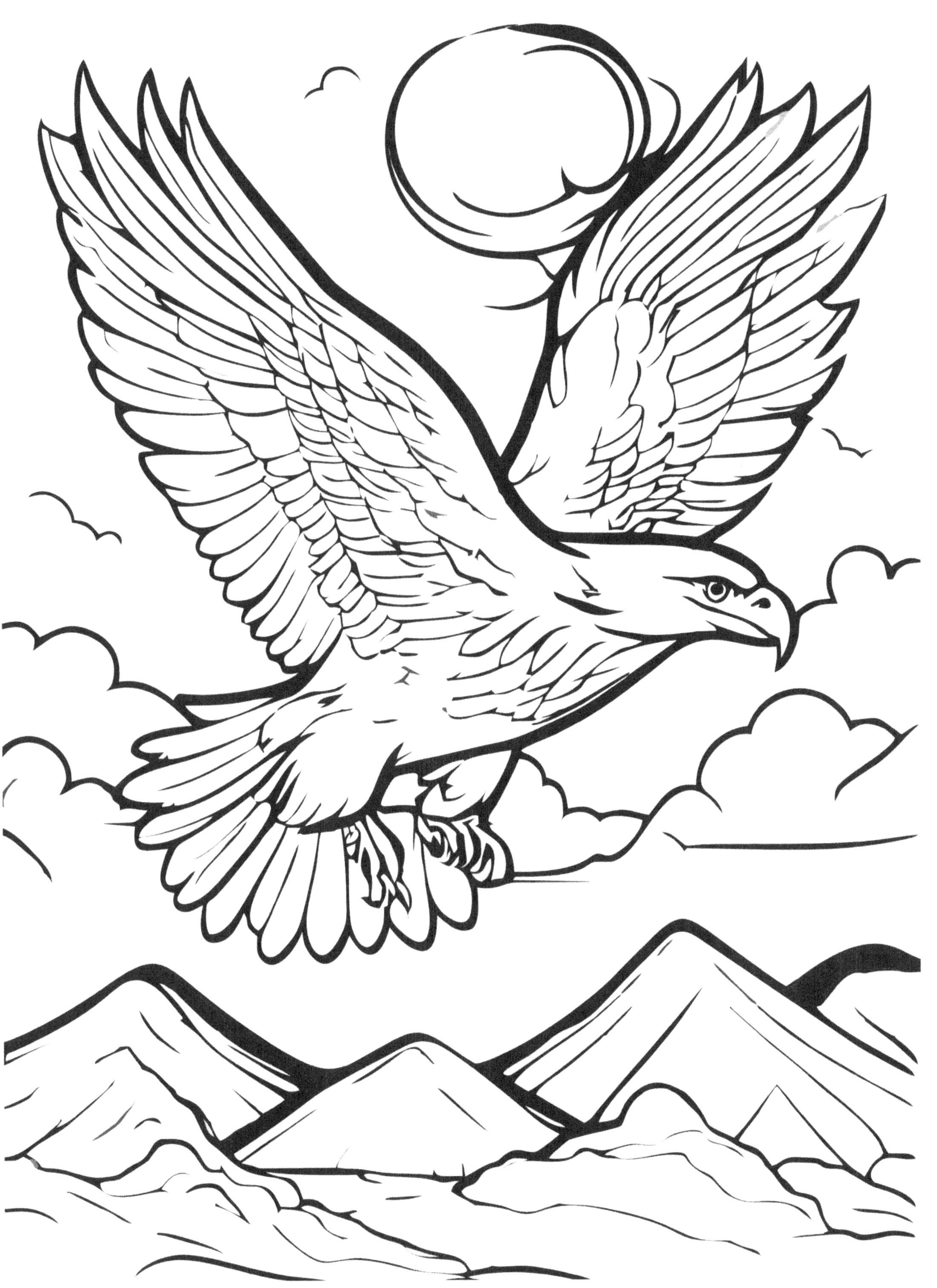

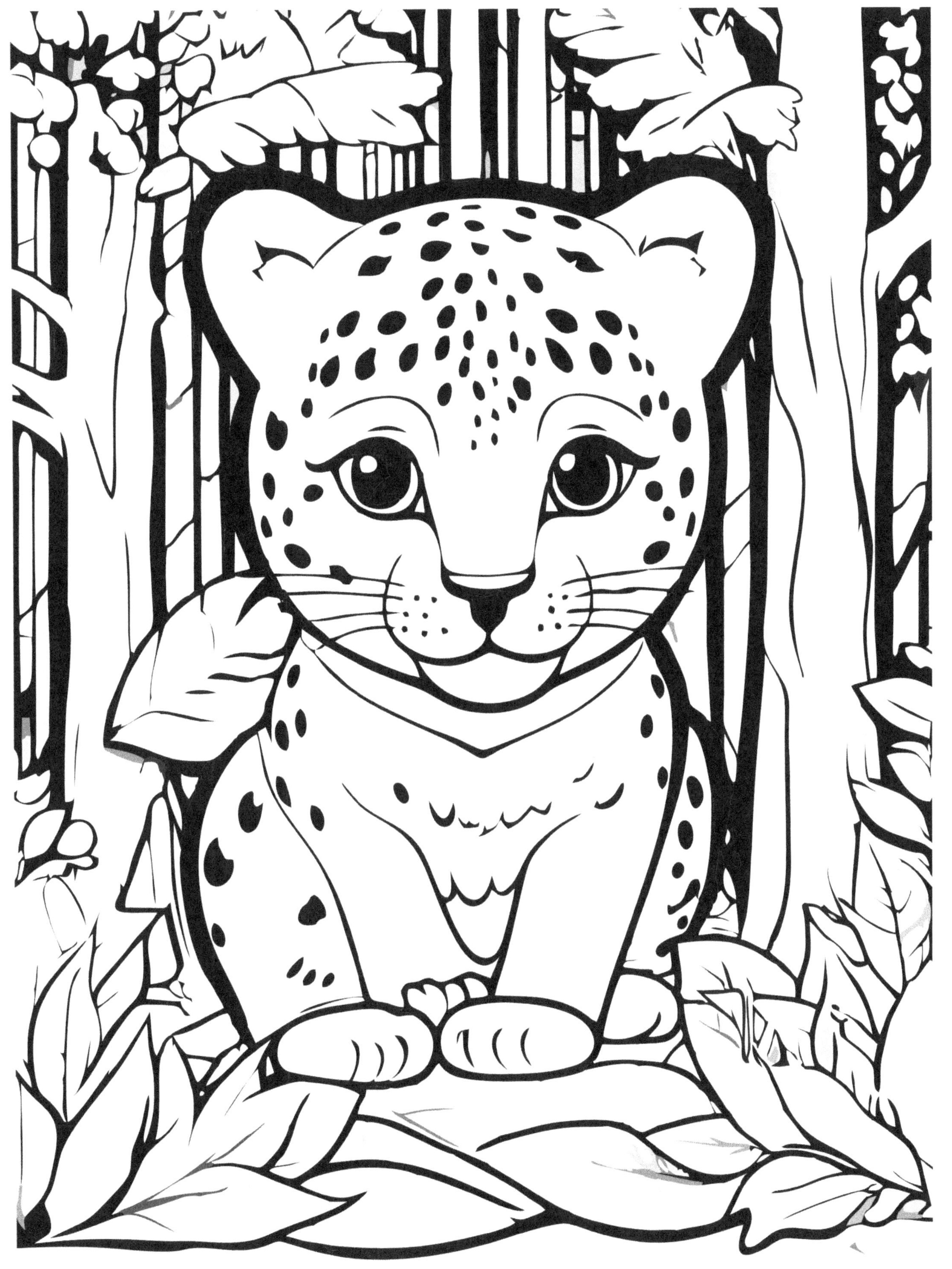

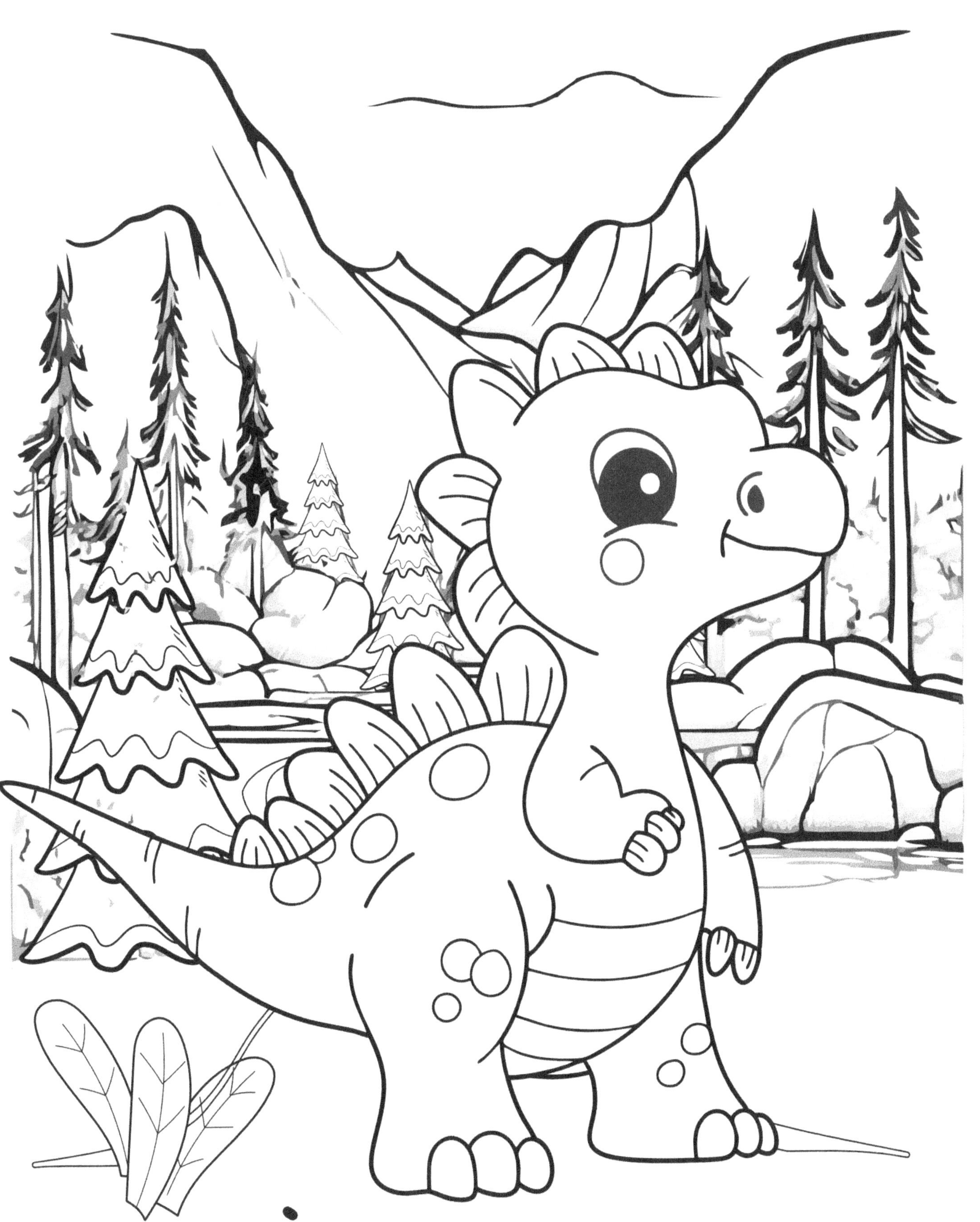

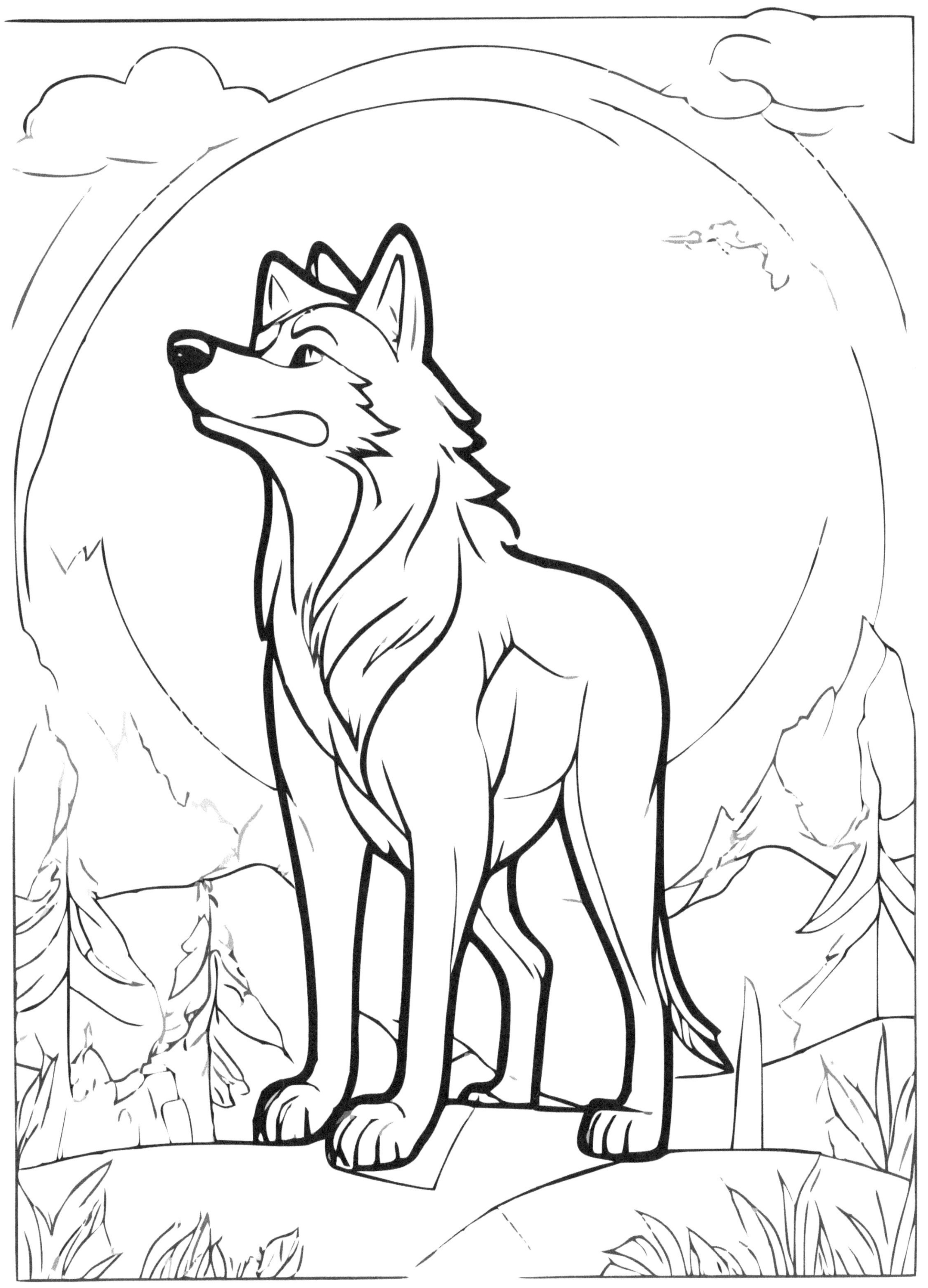

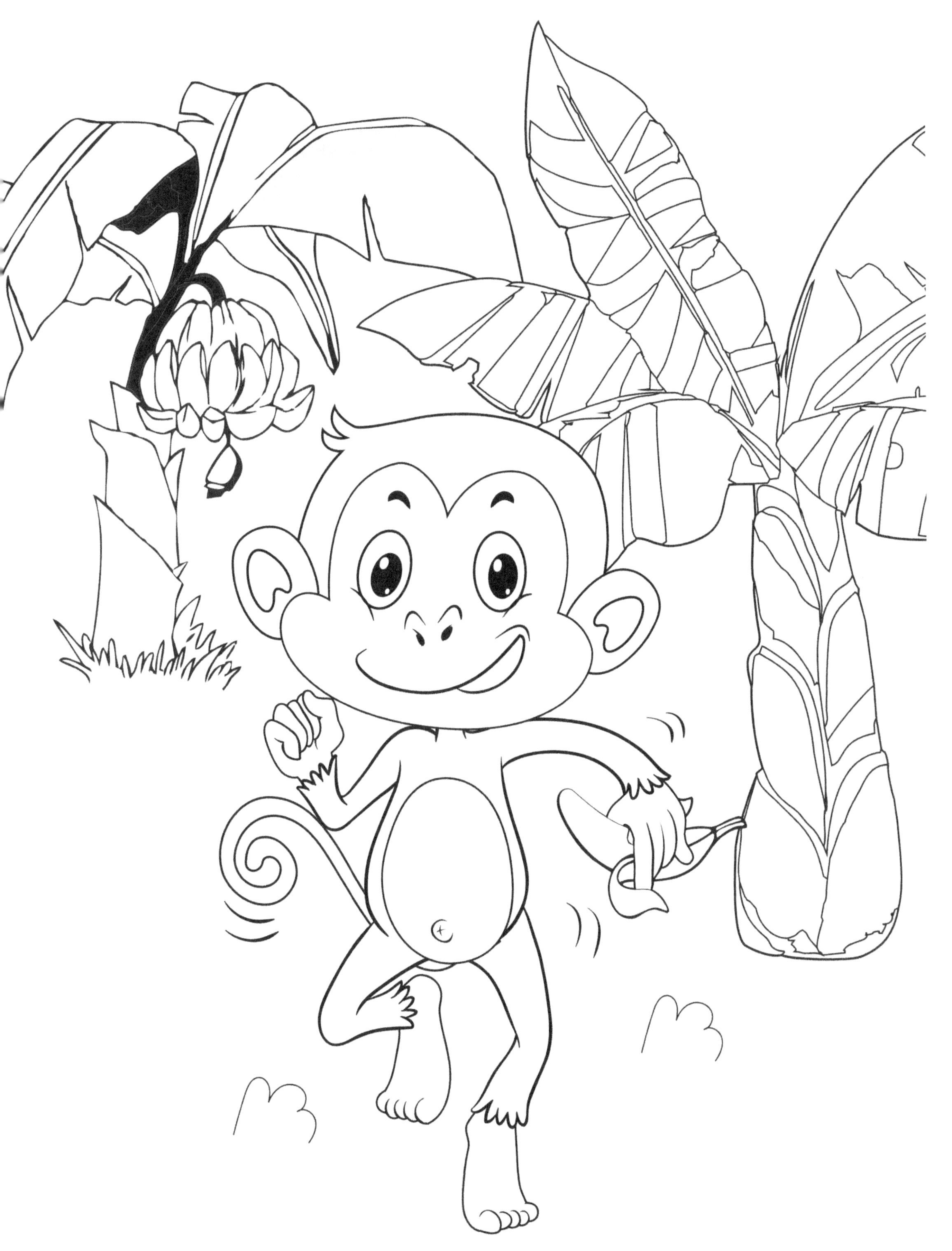

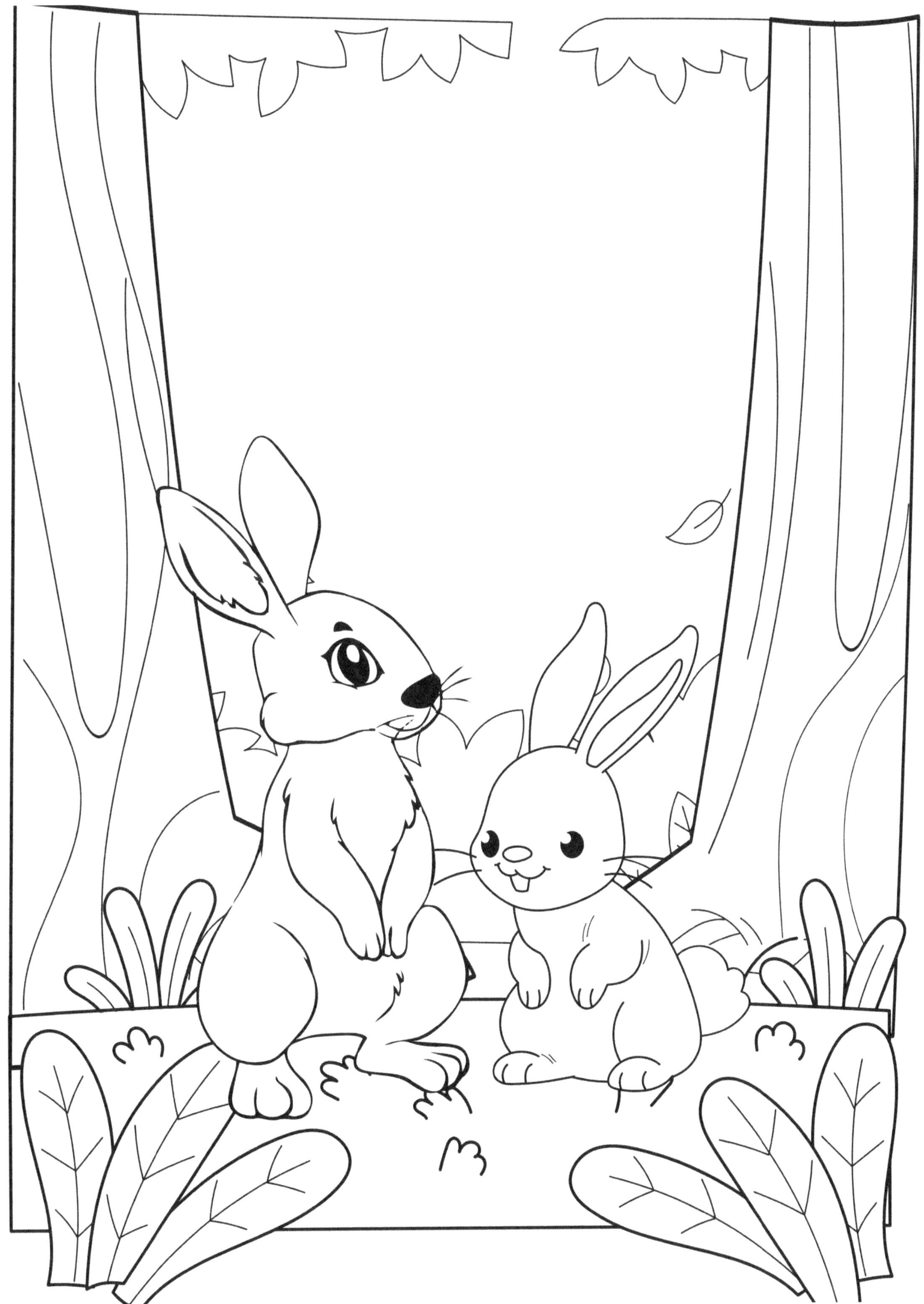

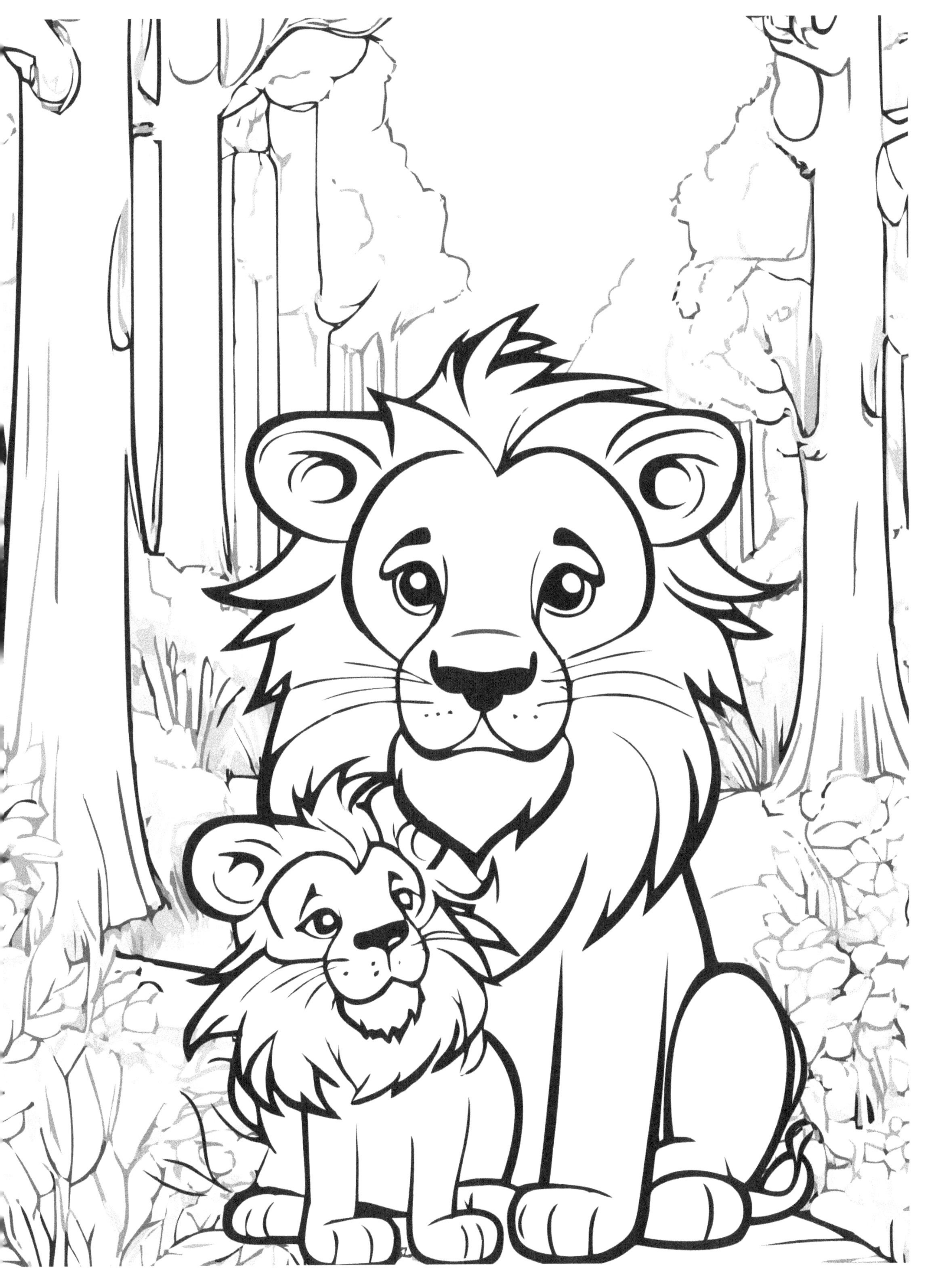

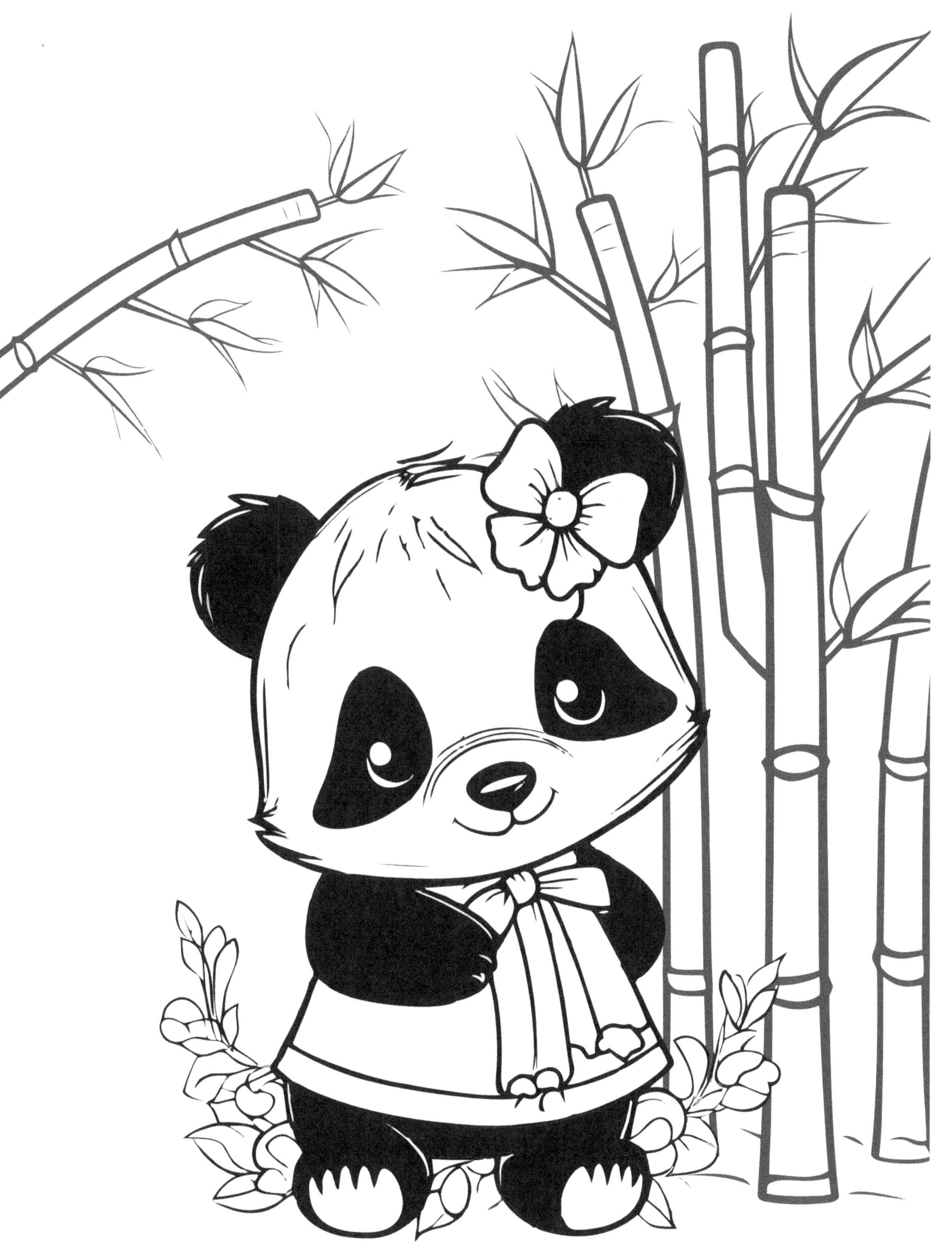

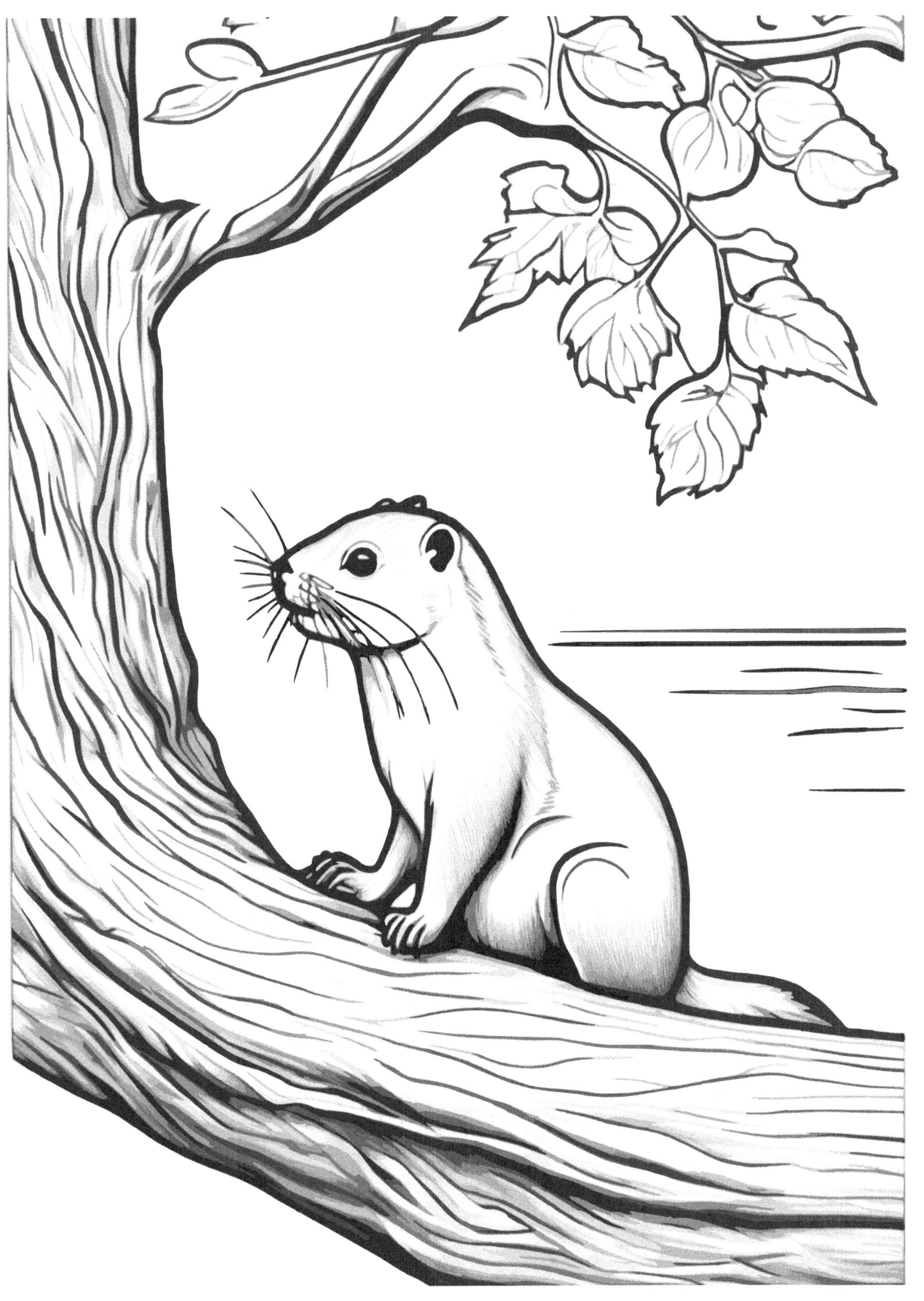

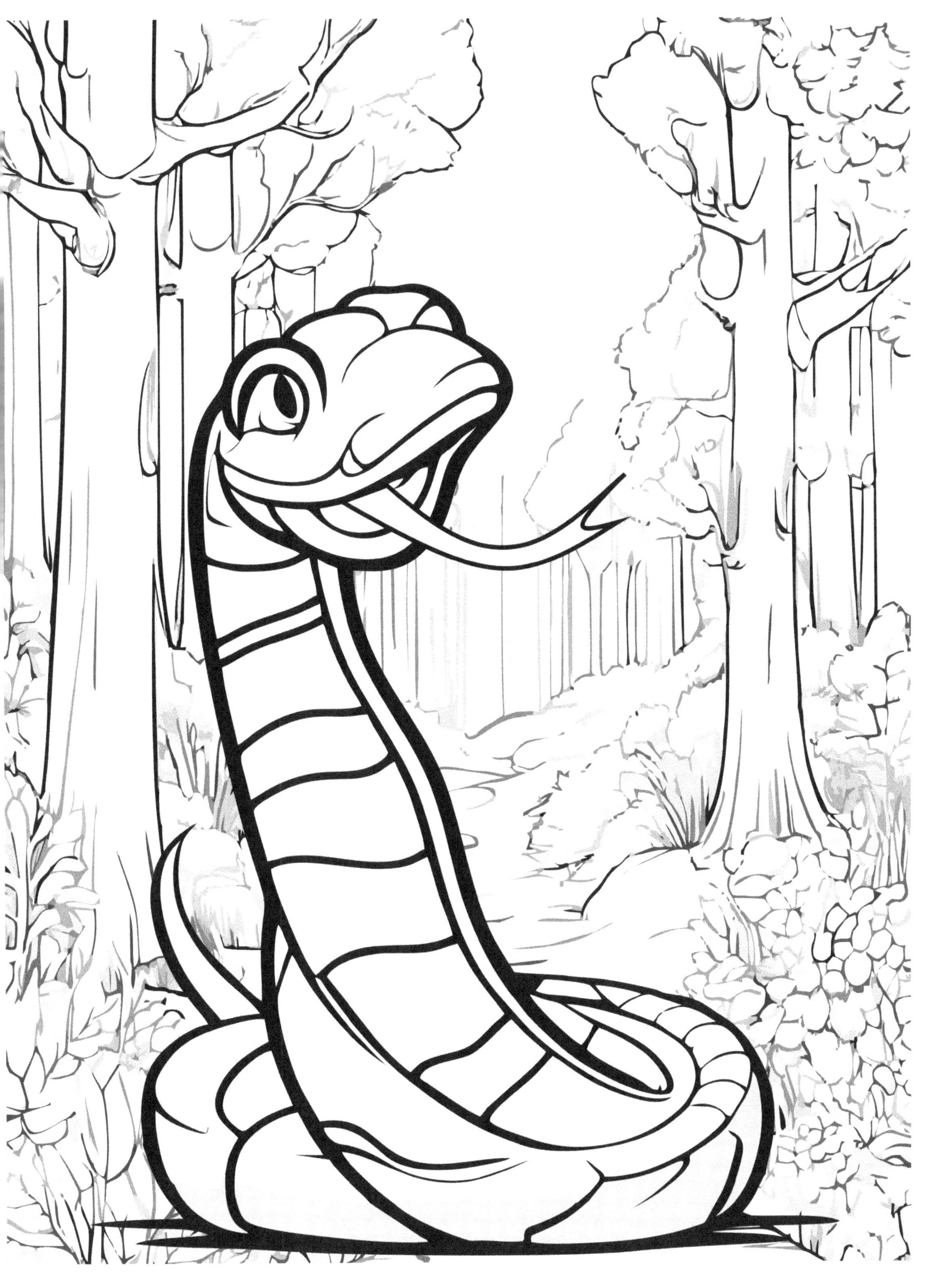

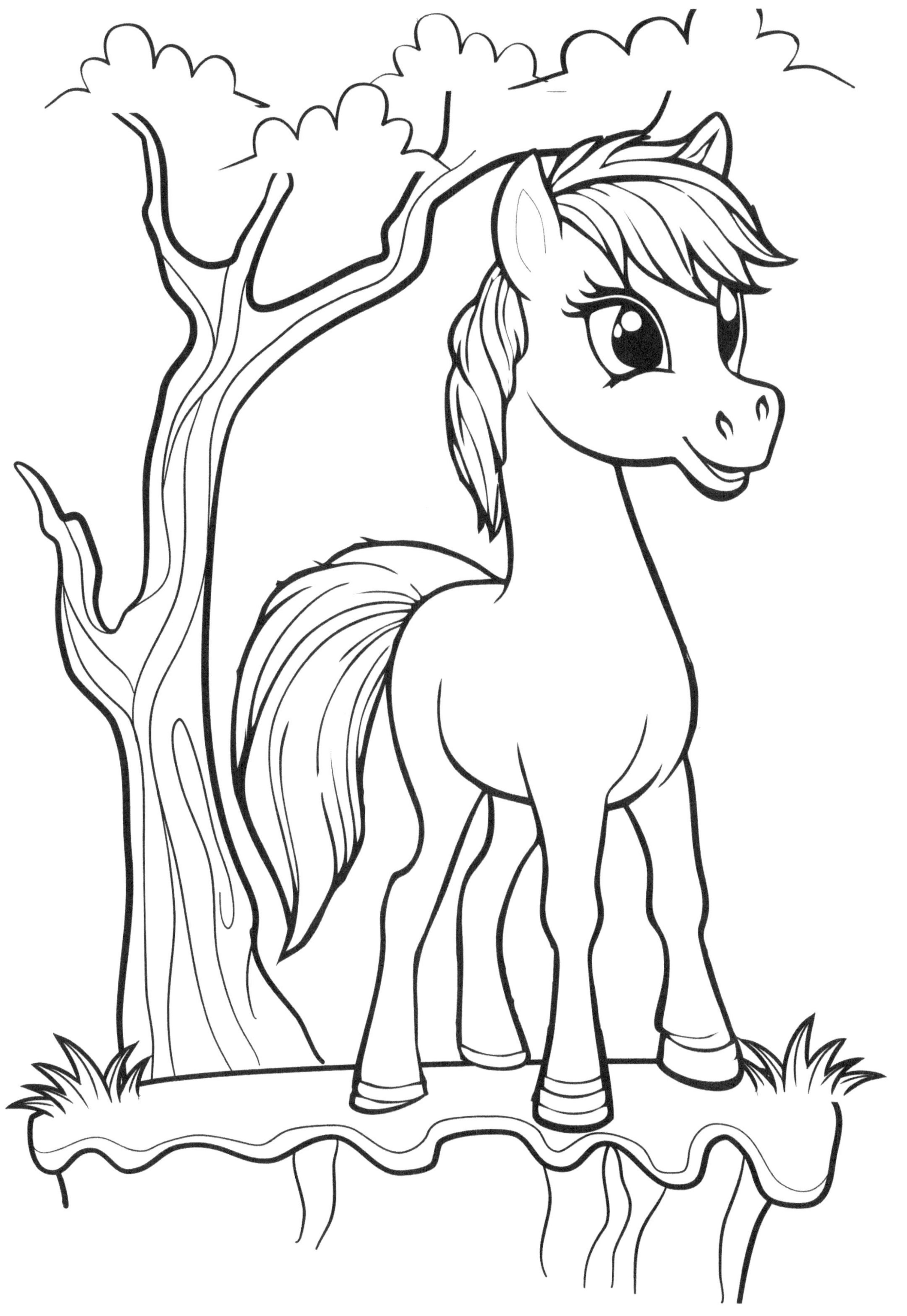

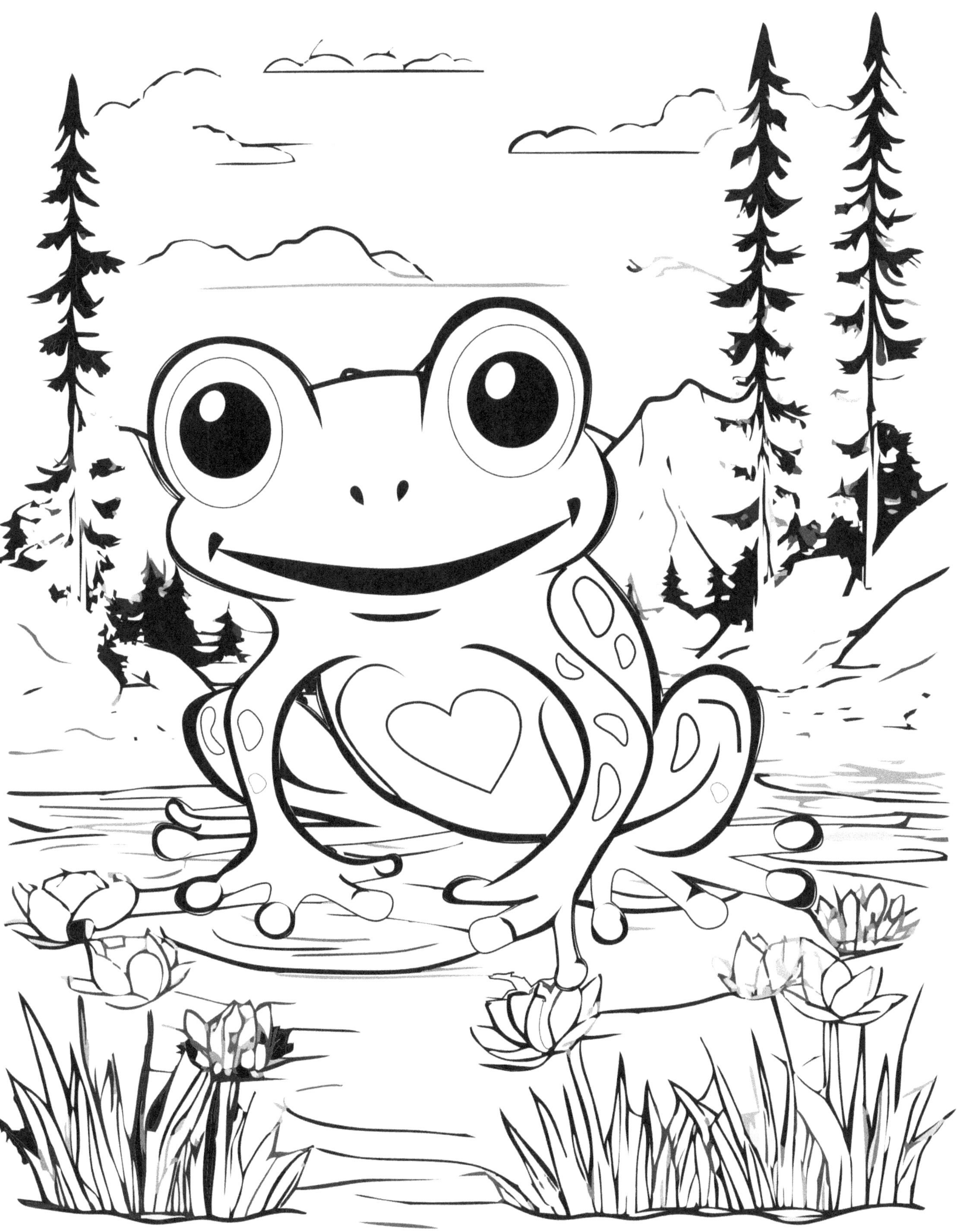

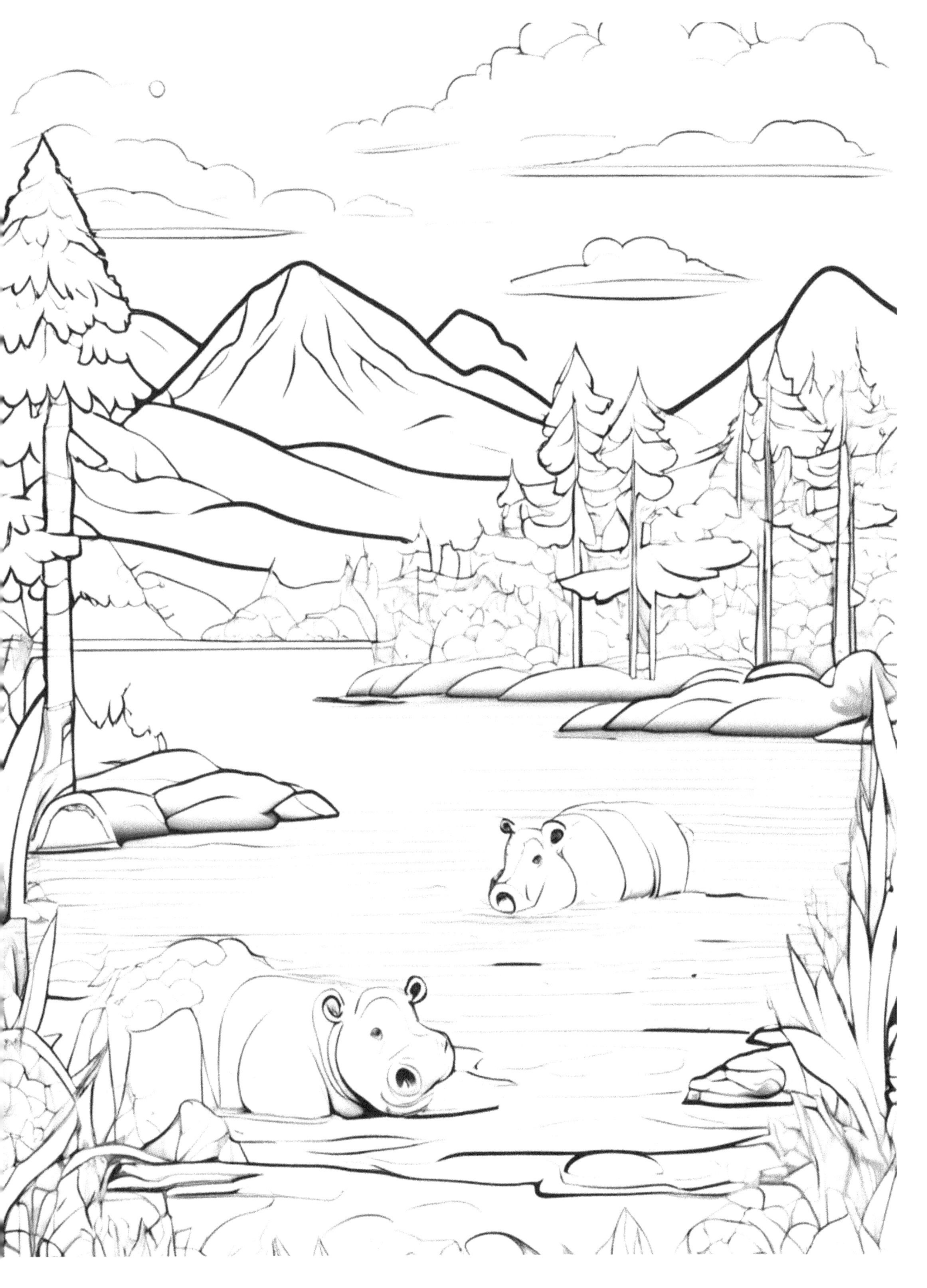

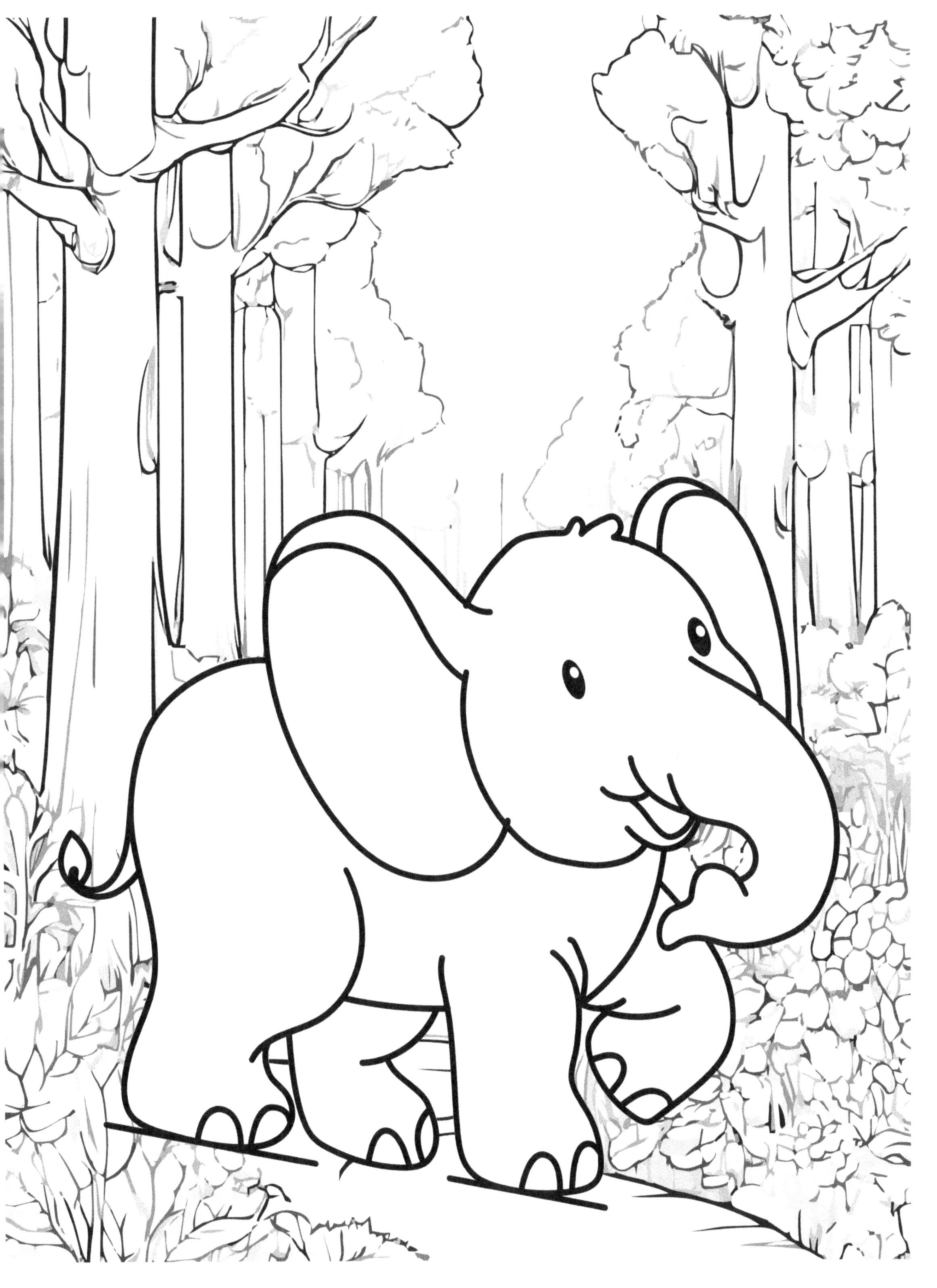